Dialogue #4

The Philosophical Equations of Economics

Chris Angle

ISBN 0-9661126-3-6
Library of Congress Catalog Number: 2001 130051

Philosophy Publishing Company
P.O. Box 708
Redding, CT 06896
Tel. 203/253-2008
Fax 203/286-2356
E-mail: chrisangle@aol.com

Manufactured in the United States of America

Other works by Christopher Angle:

Dialogue #1

The Nature of Aesthetics

Dialogue #2

Defining Ethics Good & Evil

Dialogue #3

Truth & the Nature of Decisions

The Philosophic Equations of Economics

Table of Contents

PREFACE:

The first few pages of Chapter One are a review stemming from the two previous published dialogues (Defining Ethics Good & Evil and Truth and the Nature of Decisions) and it may leave the reader a bit perplexed in the initial subject matter, but the confusion soon dissipates with the introduction of the original equation of what equals a Sacrifice just a few pages henceforward.

The Philosophic Equations of Economics

Haskell and Detmar are characters from three previous dialogues, the subjects of which were aesthetics, ethics, truth, and the nature of decisions. The proceedings in this interview remain the same as in the other dialectics, and we find again, the graduate student, Haskell, repairing to the office door of Detmar, a botany professor, at the university where they are situated. This time Haskell has a new set of problems for Detmar which have precipitated out of Haskell's review of the last conversation on truth, and the nature of decisions .

Chapter One - A Review of the Nature of a Decision

Haskell appears at the office doorway of Detmar, knocks, and the following transpires.

Haskell: Professor!

Detmar: Haskell, how are you?

Haskell: Good, thanks. How are you? It's been a while. Sorry I haven't dropped by since the interview we had on truth and the nature of decisions, but I have been busy.

Detmar: I'm sure. What have you been up to?

Haskell: Well, of course, my studies in philosophy, but also, I use the subject matter of our conversations to fulfill some of my philosophy course requirements, and I have actually transcribed our latest interchange into book form.

Detmar: Very good. I hope I have been instrumental in advancing your philosophical understandings.

Haskell: Yes. Each disquisition has answered my questions, and I believe each of the transcriptions has comprehensively elucidated answers to the essences of aesthetics, ethics, and truth.

Detmar: It is very nice of you to say so.

Haskell: Not at all. It keeps me coming back for more and today is no different.

Detmar: Oh? You have something on your mind?

Haskell: Yes. Very much so.

Detmar: Well, what is it? I am very interested to hear it.

Haskell: Upon review of our last two conversations there is something that is not clear and settled in my mind. I remember, when we spoke of the nature of ethics, we proposed that all of life runs on free will, risk, effort, and sacrifice. Then, in the subsequent interview on the essence of truth we examined the nature of a decision by which all of life's behavior must operate.

Detmar: Yes.

Haskell: Well, I am unable to integrate both statements. That is, first you stated that all of life runs on free will, risk, effort, and sacrifice, and in addition, you stated that all of life's decisions are composed of reason, effort, information, priorities, and an action.

Detmar: Yes, I did.

Haskell: Well, it seems that you have two explanations for the function of decision making.

Detmar: I see your problem.

Haskell: This is important to me because if we can clarify these two statements and come to a unified understanding of how life operates on the behavioral level, then I plan to subsequently draw you into a second set of interrogatives aimed at extrapolating some further significance with respect to our conclusions in the area of economics.

Detmar: That sounds interesting.

Haskell: Well to begin, perhaps we could start by iterating the standard or definition of a decision or the essence of how all life behaves.

Detmar: We may recall from our last conversation that the process by which all behavior in life operates is by the mechanics of the decision process which takes place in the consciousness as all life is sentient. Without consciousness there is death. Consciousness is the vehicle by which the entropic may go to the anti-entropic.

Haskell: Yes, I remember.

Detmar: Further, as consciousness is the arena where free will and information (which is memory retained experience) convene and are powered by life's anti-entropic energy, any diminishment or empowerment of these parameters will correspondingly shrink or expand the consciousness. Thus, for example, if we increase our knowledge, we expand our consciousness. If we add to the intensity of the free will parameter which has the components of reason and life's effort as we previously discussed, again, the consciousness increases.

Haskell: I agree. If we add to the ingredients or increase their intensity, we add to the general size or scope of the thing. We, Homo sapiens, have a greater consciousness than lower forms of life due to our increased knowledge and our ability to reason. And, I suppose, our collective earthly consciousness may not be the greatest in the universe as there may exist other life elsewhere in the galaxies and its overall intelligence may be greater than our own, and hence, its corresponding consciousness would also be greater. It goes without saying that our creator would have the supreme consciousness which is probably omniscient.

Detmar: We can state that the more one can experience, the greater is the consciousness, and the less we experience, the less we have consciousness. And so, if in your life, suddenly, you loose the occasion or capacity to experience something like going to the library, going to visit your girl friend, or just the ability to experience anything that you could, previously, you have a decrease in your consciousness. Moreover, if you loose the capacity for memory, consciousness will again decrease as memory is a governing parameter. When one of the limiting parameters of the consciousness is decreased or lost, we are actually undergoing a partial death. And of course, when there is total loss of consciousness, we have total death.

Haskell: That's interesting. This statement seems to indicate that should we loose some capacity of the consciousness or if we have a decrease in any of the factors that make up the consciousness, we are actually undergoing death. For example, if I were to loose the capacity to memorize my studies, or if I were senile and no longer able to remember things in the present and recent past, this lack of mental capacity would actually be an edging toward death.

Detmar: Yes.

Haskell: However, if I were to break up with my girl friend or she were to tell me that she did not want to see me any more, then this lack of experience, too, would be an incremental form of death.

Detmar: Yes.

Haskell: Well, I think I understand the loss of memory example, but I am not sure about whether the diminishment of experience would be a partial or incremental death of the consciousness. That is, if I were to get into a situation whereby the quantity of experiences decreases and I am left with less incoming stimuli for some reason or another, then I would be experiencing less, and therefore, a corresponding degree of death would be about me.

Detmar: Yes, that is the situation.

Haskell: I am not sure I can agree. It seems to me that in this situation the vivaciousness of the consciousness still exists as it did before, it is just that the incoming stimuli is less and so the consciousness does not have as much raw material as before to work with. It would seem that this is just boredom and that the consciousness is just as full of life as before and that all the ingredients of the consciousness generated by the life energy, or the anti-entropic energy, would need to disappear before any kind of death would overcome us.

Detmar: The ingredients of the consciousness are the rational faculties, which are a kind of the interior originating experiences, plus effort, memory, the life force's anti-entropic energy, and experiences in general. Without any one of these there can be no consciousness. It is like an assembly line whereby everything is in place ready to produce something, but there is no product moving down the line. The work is stopped; there is no raw material entering at one end and no final product rolling off at the other end. If the line is not operating, it is down; it is not alive, it is dead. Again, a gun without a bullet is non-operational and not worth anything. A consciousness without experience is non-operational.

Haskell: But my objection is when the experience is

diminished. The consciousness seems just as alive when there is less or little experience rolling through it.

Detmar: It is alive but less alive as there is less coming off the consciousness' assembly line. Its overall essence, if quantified, would be less and therefore, I put forth the idea that it moves toward death and that the lost part is a dead part, lost to our life and consciousness. We could say that the intensity of the consciousness would be less.

Haskell: But the decreasing of the intensity of experiences is not an edging toward death. It seems to me that the consciousness receives the experiences and assimilates them for life's purposes of producing offspring and goods and services on its way to surviving and bringing itself as far away from misery as possible.

Detmar: That is an excellent outline of the situation, but without interior originating experiences coming to the consciousness you have death. I think you will agree. You do not believe that a decrease of the incoming stimuli diminishes the intensity of the consciousness.

Haskell: Yes, that is true because the anti-entropic

force within us generates our internal experiences, and without this there is certainly death.

Detmar: Yes, and that is physical death. It is the end of us in this world. The loss of good exterior originating experiences is not of a physical death, but perhaps we should say we are undergoing a mental or symbolic death. When we recognize that we have the loss of a set of good experiences from without, our consciousness will respond with sorrow, and in some severe cases we cry. It is mental pain that we suffer when we realize that a set of good experiences is no longer available to us. And this loss is a death of sorts. Let us not call it a physical death in its entirety, but it is a mental or spiritual death because it is a loss of consciousness.

Haskell: And you have used the word "good" here to mean those experiences that promote our survival?

Detmar: Yes.

Haskell: OK. Let me move to the point which started this tangent to the conversation which is that I have a problem assimilating this with your statement from our discussion on ethics which noted that all life runs on risk, effort, sacrifice, and free will. When you stated that life "runs on" something, I assume that you referred to life's decisions which include its resultant actions. So as we live day to day, we take in our experiences, assimilate them, apply our rational faculties (which gives us our information and knowledge) using as a reference our priorities, which is previously established knowledge, to initiate an action which will hopefully help us negotiate our way through our predicament.

Detmar: Yes.

Haskell: So still, I cannot see how the twain shall meet here.

Detmar: The first statement is a description of us in our predicament. It encompasses the situation of the consciousness, its incoming stimuli, and the need for us to initiate an action to obtain a result.

Haskell: So, it includes something more than just a decision?

Detmar: Yes, it indicates our decision making amidst our predicament. The free will is a common element in both statements and obviously not an issue.

Haskell: However, you have essentially used effort

twice: free will includes reason plus effort.

Detmar: Effort is needed as a component of free will as we need to make an effort to utilize our rational faculties, but we also need effort at the physical level too in order to provide the attendant action resultant of the decision.

Haskell: Alright. How about risk? I realize that risk in our environment abounds everywhere and the information that we receive about it is requisite for us to consider, or we would soon perish.

Detmar: Risk information resides within the stimuli that come to us, and this information, as you just pointed out, is necessary for our well-being. We welcome this information as we need to reduce this miasma of risk at every step.

Haskell: And lastly, sacrifice.

Detmar: Sacrifice is the completion of the entire composite event to effectuate the consummation of the fulfillment of the decisional priority.

Haskell: Well, I'm not sure still how to integrate these two statements: is it that the first, mentioned in our ethics disquisition, is imprecise, or is it that it is a generalization which invokes vagueness?

Detmar: It is a general description of our situation. The decisional statement is narrower in scope and fits within our general statement. Our description of a decision as free will, knowledge, priorities, and an action describes life's decision making process which it needs to negotiate its way through life. Our first statement is greater in time and composition: it indicates the incoming stimuli producing experience but additionally denotes the importance of risk, free will, and the effort of the resultant physical action to obtain a desired goal which is the sacrifice. The factor of time is, of course, understood.

Haskell: Perhaps the best way to obtain an integrated understanding of the statements would be to combine them. That way, I think, the two would become self-explanatory.

Detmar: The statement would be Time multiplied by Risk times Effort times Information equals the Sacrifice.

Haskell: What? What is that?

Detmar: It is an integrated statement of the decision making process. All decisions along with their consummations are thusly described.

Haskell: It sounds to me like a third statement, and I do not mind saying that it is confusing more than enlightening.

Detmar: The two previous statements were just lists of the ingredients of a decision in the context of an application to life's situation. This new statement indicates not only ingredients but also the process of the decision and its predicament.

Haskell: Well, let's analyze it. What happened to free will?

Detmar: Recalling our previous conversation on truth, free will is our rational faculties plus a mental energy, and it loads the equation that drives the process.

Haskell: Maybe you could explain the whole statement.

Detmar: Gladly. First, the whole decision making process is called a sacrifice.

Haskell: Yes, I remember this concept from our talk on ethics.

Detmar: Every action that life does is a sacrifice to attain some goal. Whatever our intention, we must make a sacrifice to attain it. This is true for the most difficult objectives such as making a living in a tough world, raising a family, or to the obtaining of the simplest of pleasures such as reaching for a bit of dessert. In every case a sacrifice of effort is made to attain an objective even when it is pure pleasure. To enjoy a piece of dessert we had to go to work, get paid, go to the grocery store, prepare and consume the meal, and finally, we have the opportunity to enjoy the dessert. The whole process right up to the actual pleasure of tasting the dessert (the reward) is the sacrifice. The sacrifice equals those tribulations and time spent up to the point of the desired pleasure, for it is pleasure that we all ultimately desire in every situation as noted by Plato and is the culmination of all effort. I call this situation, the Sacrifice. This Sacrifice equals the culmination of the effort and time spent in every situation in all of life.

Haskell: As I understand it, the Sacrifice equals the Reward, and hence, they are the same thing. But it does not seem to me that a sacrifice is a reward.

Detmar: They are on the opposite sides of the equation, and they equal each other. The Sacrifice is all the time and effort spent in the face of risk and the culmination of this is the reward. The dessert, or that is, the Reward, is the result of all the effort and time that went into the making of the dessert.

Haskell: I think you have confused or overlapped two related things: first you have tried to quantify the modulatory operations of decision making; but then just now, you equated or expanded this to include the actual production of something - in this case, the dessert - and of course, you must include capital in order to make something. Every economic text will inform us that capital and labor together are needed to produce something.

Detmar: Yes, thank you. You are absolutely right. As we have defined things so far, we are just indicating a mental decision to obtain the reward of the dessert which is the result of Time multiplied by Risk times Effort times Information. This equation, let's write it as R X T X I X E = The Sacrifice, represents a decision to perform an action. If we want to let it cover the production of something, then we need, as you pointed out, to include capital and the tools we use that combine with the effort that will enable us to not only decide to do something but also to produce it.

Haskell: And how would you describe the new

equation?

Detmar: We would say that Time multiplied by Risk times Information times Physical Effort times Capital (or as some economists might say, Land) equals the Reward, or that is, the Product. To put it succinctly we might write it as

T X R X I X (E(physical) X Land) = The Reward

The reward is the material manifestation of the general sacrifice. When we speak of the Sacrifice, we are referring to the actions consequent of life's decisions; and as to the reward there are the specific things that are produced as a result of the actions of the sacrifice.

Haskell: We are traveling too fast, and now that I understand that there is a difference between the Sacrifice and Reward and that a Reward is a consequence of the Sacrifice, let's slow down and go back to the first equation and examine it a little more as I do not yet understand it completely.

Detmar: Surely.

Haskell: First, you stated that (R)(E)(T)(I) = The Sacrifice, but tell me about how free will has been woven into this equation of the decision.

Detmar: In our previous interview on truth, decisions, and free will we noted that free will is our rational faculties plus effort. When we make, or that is, when all of life makes a decision, it makes an effort to use its rational abilities. But specifically, it applies its rational capacity to the risk information that it receives from without, to the experience of time, and to the general information and knowledge of the situational predicament. This would be the nature of a mental decision.

Haskell: Wait. What happened to the priority?

Detmar: In the basic decision where there is yet to be effected a physical action, the reward is the priority.

Haskell: How's that?

Detmar: Our first step to a decision is the establishment of a priority which becomes an objective when the relevant circumstances arise. When we decide that we want to go to the store to get something for dinner we have already made the priority that going to the store is important to alleviate the oncoming feeling of hunger. We establish the priority then effectuate it with a physical action. We make a mental effort of assimilating the time, the risk, and the general information to establish the priority of going to the store. And this sacrifice of the mental effort to establish a priority produces the reward of a priority.

Haskell: How could a priority be construed as a reward?

Detmar: It is a reward because it unclutters the mind. We need priorities to order our lives. They are the likes, the dislikes, the do's and the don'ts. We need them in order to know for ourselves how to live. We sacrifice mental effort in combination with information, both interiorly and exteriorly originating, to establish these priorities, and they are rewards in themselves as they are needed to order our lives.

Haskell: I see. But here in our simple equation of the mental effort, which is a sacrifice to establish the reward of a priority, how do we know to use multiplication in combining the factors of time, information, risk, and effort?

Detmar: We know because it produces consistent and integrated results.

Haskell: Really?

Detmar: We can see that the factors of time, information, and risk cannot be added together because they are different entities and have different consistencies. Time is described differently from information and risk. Time is in seconds (or another unit of time), information is described by degrees of the incoming phenomena, and risk would be noted by a probability factor which could be written in terms of a percentage. These various factors cannot be added together. It would not make sense.

Haskell: Why not? After all, the terms of time and risk are both forms of knowledge or information. We would be just adding different forms of information together. We would just be adding together risk information, time information, and the relevant information of the situation together.

Detmar: Yes, you can add them together if all the factors can be known in informational terms and we do not try to differentiate them. If differentiation is not important to us, it is OK. But I think we want to analyze the individual factors, and when we do so, we will be noting each factor in its individual units such as time. We can note time to be in seconds, minutes, hours, and effort to be in, let's say, man units, or in torque, or horsepower, and information to be in bytes, and risk to be purely a mathematical percentage factor. If they were all considered forms of information, then we would have to add them as bytes or as any other dimension in which you would care to describe information.

Haskell: I think I see the result. If we choose a label and multiply them out we could get Risk (in %) X Information (in bytes) X Effort (in millivolts) X Time (in hours) = the Priority Reward (in bytes-millivolt-hours) which I believe is conceivable.

Detmar: Yes, good. Please note that the multiplication is the integral action as our equation may require other derivative processes such as the use of exponentials or logarithms.

Haskell: OK. And this equation, as just described, is for the mental decision.

Detmar: Yes.

Haskell: And I suppose that the mental faculties deposit in each slot of the equation the appropriate information. It will judge each situation to have so much risk, so much effort, and the time that will be needed; and the how to - or the engineering - information will be derived and deposited into the equation and multiplied out to give the final reward which will become a new priority.

Detmar: Yes.

Haskell: Well, what about when we effectuate this new priority and add in physical action to make it happen. Action is not in the equation.

Detmar: We need to widen the scope of the energy factor to include not only the brain energy but also physical energy. We would do this either by making a new equation which would be noted in terms, for example, of man work units, torque, or ergs instead of the millivolts that we first used. Any term (or combination of terms) that describes the type of physical labor being consummated will be appropriate.

Haskell: OK.

Detmar: Or we can just add in the new physical effort to the first equation and we would get effort in millivolts times effort in man units or in torque or in BTU's, or whatever, giving the final effort factor in mental millivolts-physical torque. The entire equation might be summarized in bytes-millivolts-torque-hours described in a percentage basis noting the probability of its effectuation being anywhere from a near sure thing to a small chance of happening.

Haskell: Well, at the beginning of this conversation I said that once we got into it, I planned to direct the conversation toward another area of interest.

Detmar: Yes.

Haskell: Well, I think it the appropriate time to do so. I have been asking these questions in order to research an understanding into social, political, and economic decision making because I believe that if we understand the nature of the decision, we can proceed to further our understandings of the economic decision, the political decision, and the nature of government. But for today's interview I will seek an understanding of the philosophy of economic decision making and its integumental concepts.

Detmar: Yes, this does sound interesting.

Haskell: Well, I believe we have just established the basis of the decision making process. I suspect that if we add in other facts of motivation whether it be economic, social, or political, we will get the special equation for each intellectual discipline.

Detmar: We have actually established the basic equation of all three types of decision making; it is just that we must further differentiate the individual factors to make it more specific and appropriate for whatever discipline we should study.

Chapter 2 - The Social Decision

Haskell: Well, let's try the social decision first since we have already studied ethics in a previous interview. So far, the equation denotes a solitary mental decision. Would a social decision differ from the equation we have already established that defines a mental decision which produces the priorities by which we order our lives?

Detmar: The criterion that defines all social decisions is cooperation as we studied in our discussion on ethics. Therefore, we must incorporate this concept into the equation.

Haskell: But, we have already established that we have a complete equation and that any changes would be through differentiation of the existing contents.

Detmar: Correct. We have within us interior originating experiences that indicate a will to respect those with whom we intend and need to cooperate for the purpose of the production that will enable us to survive: we know that the more we cooperate and produce, the farther we get from bare existence, rise toward prosperity, and take ourselves away from misery.

Haskell: We definitely want to rise above poverty and a bare subsistence level as no one likes misery.

Detmar: And we know that, except for the cerebral ascetic, to be a lone person and obtain this objective of reproducing a family, strive for a comfortable living, and stay as far away from misery as possible, cooperation with others is needed. Hardly anyone wants to do everything.

Haskell: Yes. We discussed this extensively in our discussion on ethics. We have a need to cooperate and live with the others around us to raise families that will survive us; and being a societal animal, we know that cooperation accelerates our general well-being by enabling us to produce more effectively than if we were to be by ourselves or just to live by the unit family.

Detmar: Consequently, through evolution, whether it is by theistic or naturalistic orientation (or a combination of both), we can recognize that there is an inherent urge for us to cooperate. We enjoy being cooperative and prefer to be societal (except for the true ascetic who has a different agenda probably tending to mental purity), and this experience of ours to be cooperative is an established priority of ours. We can place its presence in the equation within the factor of effort. It is known to us, whether the experience is biologically communicated or through cultural indoctrination or both, and we realize that we need and want to cooperate, and early on we establish this as a prime priority by which we should live. We establish that, first, we want to cooperate with others, and then, we choose with whom we shall cooperate.

Haskell: OK. I agree that information comes to us probably both from within and without in combination, that we need to be cooperative with others, and actually, I know from within me that I want to cooperate with others for the purpose of my own particular objectives which I suppose I could say are my established priorities. I want to cooperate with my professors to succeed in absorbing the academic tasks sufficiently to obtain the accolades in order to achieve the degree from the university. After that, I imagine that I will want to cooperate with those with whom I will work in a job that will allow me to receive remuneration to live my life. Of course, I am not sure what my compensatory goals are yet, as my own personal objectives of how I want to live have not congealed and quantified in my mind, but I do know that I certainly need enough to be able to live respectfully in society; and maybe, should I ever find the girl who could put up with me, I would take the plunge and get married although at this point that seems such a farfetched idea. But I accede to your position and to the point that we made in our discussion on ethics that the culminant objective of our impetus to cooperate is production which allows us to fly from misery.

Detmar: Yes.

Haskell: But where in the equation does this need and desire to cooperate lie? It would seem to be within the factor of information as it seems that the will and urge to cooperate come mostly from internally originating phenomena, but, of course, some may be from without. But in any case it seems to be in the form of incoming stimuli to the consciousness and that would qualify it - if I remember and understand our discussion on truth, knowledge, and free will correctly - as information and then knowledge.

Detmar: Good. A priority, once established, is a type of knowledge that we use to order our lives. And we should remember what you pointed out that actually all our factors within the decisional equations are within the realm of information and that even includes the effort factor. All are types of stimuli coming to the consciousness, such as, the feeling of time, or the sense of risk that lies in every predicament we come across in our daily lives; even the feeling of effort comes to the consciousness as stimuli and is a form of information. However, we know that we can differentiate further through analysis by our free will the different and major forms of this information for purposes of understanding the nature of a decision better. However, its very core is information plus our free will plus an action.

Haskell: And how should we express this factor of cooperation within our equation of the decision?

Detmar: This factor would be dimensionless and would be expressed purely mathematically as a coefficient of the effort factor. Hence, as it is probability, it would be (Risk X (c)Effort X Time) X Information which would equal the Sacrifice.

Haskell: And would this cover any decision that we might make in the social arena?

Detmar: Yes.

Haskell: How about a couple of examples such as when we are working in a company and we need to cooperate with our co-workers to produce something that consumers or manufacturers or service companies value and want to purchase, or when we are married and we are cooperating with our wife to procreate children, bring them up, and educate them.

Detmar: When we work with others in the work place, we have already established as a priority through the decisional process that one needs to produce something, whether good or service, in return for which we will receive compensation that we may use to acquire goods and services that allow us to lift ourselves up from a subsistence level lifestyle and away from misery.

Haskell: Yes.

Detmar: When we cooperate, we do so by several working as one toward the same specific goal with the objective being the Reward in our equation. The Priority, a piece of knowledge, is already established and visible by the fact that one is at work, producing, and the Risk and Time of the situation remain as they are. This cooperation, when two or more work toward a common goal, indicates the purely mathematical function of multiplication of effort. Hence, in our equation a coefficient of the effort factor satisfies this requirement.

Haskell: I see.

Detmar: The same is true of the confluence of a man and woman becoming husband and wife to issue offspring. The common objective is the production of children to survive the parents and they work as one to this goal. Hence, there is a common objective which is the Reward produced by the Sacrifice, the content of which is time, risk, information/knowledge, and a cooperative effort, for without the cooperation the goal is impossible.

Haskell: Well technically then, it is not strictly speaking purely a mathematical function of effort such as the doubling of effort, but two individual separate efforts combined together.

Detmar: True. If you differentiate the purposes of the man and the woman into separate forms of effort, then there is an additional dimension to this effort, but the coefficient does not disappear, it remains to indicate efficiency. The equation should be written as Time X Risk X Coefficient of Effort (a) times Effort (b) equals the Sacrifice which equals the Reward, that is, (R X T) X c(Ea X Eb) = Reward.

Haskell: Hence, any social situation would be

completely described by this equation. I suppose we don't really need to differentiate to sexual differences if we keep our dimensional analysis as before in terms of man-hours. We would note the difference in effort only if we further differentiate the dimensional analysis to woman-man-hours.

Detmar: Yes. The equations could get as complicated, detailed, or subdivided as we wish, as we could further analyze the subcomponents of the major factors of the equational expression.

Haskell: What about wrongdoing? Is this covered? Or what about the occurrence of evil?

Detmar: Yes, they are because these are objectives. Any goal lies in the Reward, and this question is one of ethics, and we previously discussed this.

Haskell: Yes, we did. But I feel we have left out an ingredient because there is a source of evil, or for that matter, any aberrant behavior, and since the decision to do anything comes from somewhere, I do not really see where in our equation is the nature of the impetus to set up an objective - evil, bad, good, or whatever.

Detmar: All objectives are first priorities which are produced by the admixture of previously established priorities, incoming information (either in the form of interior originating experiences or exterior originating phenomena), and the free will which is composed of the rational faculties and internal mental effort all meeting in the arena of the consciousness. This free will manufactures the new priorities by which we live and the nature of how this is accomplished, that is, the nature of the life force, is yet unknown.

Haskell: Then, it seems that all behavioral differences between individuals originate in the arena of the consciousness where the incoming stimuli convene with the free will. I am interested in the problem of why people are different and why there is so much diversity of opinion. Even if we have the same education, people come up with different opinions about even the simplest of things. In looking at our equation I see that basically - or that is, in general - we all strive for the same thing such as happiness and comfort and to get away from misery (for ourselves, that is, as it seems that some of us do not mind inflicting it upon others). But upon consideration of the particular and as we become more specific, we get the divergence of objective. Do you suppose that if all individuals are given the same incoming stimuli, they would produce the same outcome, the same opinions, or the same objectives?

Detmar: Of course not. All we have to do is look at the ingredients of our equation to see that the free will parameter cannot be the same within each individual. The mental faculties within us are always different from person to person. Our ability to perceive and understand the incoming phenomena to our consciousness obviously varies within us.

Haskell: Yes, this is obviously true. Let me now ask whether there is any difference between the equation that indicates the mental decision to do something and the physical election to do something.

Detmar: What do you mean?

Haskell: We can mentally decide to do something yet not take any physical action to do it. It seems to me that in one case we decide that we will do something, however we have not yet proceeded to execute the decision with a physical action which would be the "effort" of the equation, yet in making a decision we have used mental "effort" but the equation has not yet indicated that there is a difference between mental and physical effort.

Detmar: If there is not manifestation of the physical component of the effort parameter, then the equation indicates the production of a priority - a byte of knowledge - that shall be the standard by which the second integral component of the effort parameter, physical effort, will be executed. To wit, the physical action will be executed and it is realized that the priority is reached. The priority is the standard by which we live our lives, and as we become cognizant that our priorities our realizable, at the appropriate time we execute the physical effort to consummate the attainment of the priority.

Haskell: I see. So, if a priority of mine is to vote in an election, I know that when the circumstances arise and it becomes election day, I decide to execute the priority by performing the appropriate physical measures by walking into the voting booth and choosing the levers. Or if my priority is to get good grades, as I have already mentioned, I use my effort to read, memorize, recall, and assimilate the lessons of my professors and then attempt to perform well on the examinations.

Detmar: Precisely.

Haskell: Then, Time multiplied by Risk times Effort (mental) times Information equals a Priority (a mental sacrifice); but Time X Risk X Effort (physical) times Information equals a physical Sacrifice which equals a Reward. And the use of the physical component of the effort parameter is employed when the components indicate that the circumstances of the priority have been met and the new equation with the physical effort becomes current.

Detmar: Correct.

Haskell: And if we make a unit consistency analysis of this statement, we might say that a priority equals T(hours) X R(% of failure) X Effort(millivolts) X Information(bytes) which would make it a percentage of millivolts-hour-bytes of information and a Reward would be T(hours) X R(%) X Effort(horsepower) X Information(bytes) which would be horsepower-hour-bytes of information.

Detmar: Yes, excellent.

Haskell: Now, we spoke a bit ago about how all of the factors are forms of differentiated information. We need to go over this in detail because I am quite unclear as to what you mean, and it seems by your statement that there could be other forms of information that could be differentiated and placed into the equational expression.

Detmar: You are right. All the factors that we have noted in the expression are types of experience - even effort - as we experience the mental and physical effort that we exert in solving a problem, making a priority, or consummating a sacrifice to obtain a reward.

Haskell: So, by this statement you indicate that just the factors of effort, risk, and time are not all inclusive. In fact, I suspect the reason why we keep the nomination of information in the equation is to keep it open for further information and knowledge that might be needed to create the priority or solve the problem.

Detmar: Yes.

Haskell: By the way, I assume that solving a problem and making a priority is the same thing. I take it, that when we have a problem, the problem itself is a priority in that we have established that we must solve it.

Detmar: Correct.

Haskell: But wait. I am still quite confused and there are whole gaps in my rudimentary understanding of this subject of decision making which we studied in our previous interlocution. We need to go back and review it from the start which I think should be to iterate the nature of a decision. I hope, that a second time through, my understanding will congeal. In particular the questions that are salient in my mind are that it does not seem that our equation covers all the types of decision making and that sometimes instead of combining all the information in using multiplication to get an answer as to what we should do in a situation, we sometimes may use just one or two types of information and use it in comparison as exemplified when we might say something such as "Oh, this will take too much time or that will require too much effort to do this or that."

Detmar: First, we will iterate that the basic components of a decision are only two: free will, which we may recall is our rationality plus life's energy, and information/knowledge.

Haskell: Wait. I thought that a decision was from free will, information, a priority, plus an action.

Detmar: Yes, from the formation of the decision to its physical manifestation those are its components. However, on the mental side before its resultant action the only two components are free will (along with its component of energy or mental effort) and information/knowledge (these two concepts being as we previously discussed of the same origin).

Haskell: Yes, I remember. And a priority is a kind of knowledge, and if we consider the action as the completion or outcome of the mental decision, then, yes, the core of the decision is just the two components of free will and the information-knowledge complex.

Detmar: From this we know that when we speak of the added complexities of time or risk, the origin of these additional components must only be through the differentiation of information.

Haskell: I agree that these components are incoming stimuli to the arena of the consciousness and can be classified as informative. Of course, somehow the consciousness through its partner, the life force, can initiate our efforts that we produce, but as the experiences of our effort come to the consciousness, we know that these incoming stimuli are experiences, and thus, we can know them to be information when in memory.

Detmar: And when we speak of differentiation, we are just making sub-categories of the total information spectrum and noting the types of stimuli that are coming to the consciousness that are available to make the decisions, such as time and effort and cooperation.

Haskell: Yes.

Detmar: And if our decision is a complex one with much varied stimuli and we are able to classify and categorize this information, then we may differentiate our equation to include the various types of information.

Haskell: So the equation is not just the multiplication of risk, time, effort and information, it can be more complex with the inclusion of other categories of information.

Detmar: Yes. Until now, we have left in the factor of information in our equation only to keep the door open to the potential for the different types of information that may be present to the problem at hand and relevant to the decision. It is that we have just differentiated out of that available information noted in the equation other forms of information, such as effort and time, because in almost every problem that we encounter in our daily lives, the factors of time, effort, and risk are present. All other factors vary. But if there are other ubiquitous categories of information, we can add these to the general equation. But in the particular equation we may differentiate as to the appropriate categories and add these to the singular equation but not to the general equation.

Haskell: I see. How do we describe just the thought of "Oh, it takes too much time" as no effort is required to perform any sacrifice?

Detmar: As for the question of when we might say that something takes too much time, and that is all, we have a situation where the problem is simple and carries only the component of time, and as in this situation all the relevant information is composed of temporal factors only, we can just describe our decisional equation as effort multiplied by time equaling the Sacrifice. But time is never alone as long as we are more than just a consciousness. Because we have our corporeal being about us, it is never just a matter of time alone. At least to some extent in our corporeal and mental being there will exist a relevancy of effort and risk in facing any problem or in attaining any objective. Temporal matters may be an overriding concern in a particular problem, but never to the extent that it becomes totally alone. But even if it did, it would not effect the elements of our equation or the modular nature of decision making. The mental faculties would handle the inflow of information and place the preponderance of the temporal information into the equation and leave the other factors at the numerical value of one to make them neutral.

Haskell: So there are permanent information factors in the equation that must be there due to the nature of our existential situation, and they are free will which loads the equation and time, effort, and risk. Are they the only permanent factors? It seems that there might be more.

Detmar: How so?

Haskell: Well, for example we have basic instincts within us at all times that we would classify as interior originating experiences. Examples of such feelings would be our will to reproduce, our propensity to fall in love, or the drive to live in comfort and to get as far away from misery as possible, as we discussed, which is, as I understand it from our discussion on ethics, a prerogative for us in our existence.

Detmar: Yes. Let's take the basic instinct of reproduction: almost everybody has it, it seems, as people have been rather successful at it. This instinct pervades all that are living.

Haskell: Yes, life must reproduce to perpetuate its survival. How does this fit into the equation?

Detmar: As a priority.

Haskell: But a priority is knowledge in itself. It is previously established knowledge. As we established the nature of a priority in our disquisition on ethics, we know that a priority's ingredients are free will, information, and a value which is knowledge of the good.

Detmar: Yes.

Haskell: And if it is a previously established priority, then it is manufactured from decision making which brings me to a second interrogative point in that where does the "good" fit into this problem? How is the "good" established at all?

Detmar: It is established in the same way as any priority - in the same way as any decision. However, the personal value which is from the good is established by the free will.

Haskell: What? How's that?

Detmar: Knowledge comes to the consciousness, and if it is of a primary basic set of informational parameters, a priority may not yet be established for the situation. If so, the free will establishes it. And free will must establish it because if it does not, then the value of the good which is steeped in our need for survival will arrive and be dictated from without which, of course, would mean that our actions are predetermined. But because free will works within us, we alone establish our values based on what is best for us relevant to how we understand we should promote our own survival, the survival of those who will survive us, and our getting us as far away from misery as possible.

Haskell: But does not some experience that comes to us have good within it? Let us take for example the feeling to reproduce: it seems that there is inherent good within the experience as it comes to us because it is so strong. It is an interior originating phenomenon and, I surmise, is packed with an objective already prepackaged to give us an initiative so strong that most cannot reject it. There is no doubt that within this incoming informational stimuli there is intention to motivate the person to a specific type of behavior - in this case to reproduce. And actually, with any genetically induced feeling to set up a predisposition to initiate a certain type of behavior in the Homo sapiens or any animal, wherever there is a consciousness, there seems to be behind it a positive, good purpose. Therefore, cannot we say that here in these situations that the good already exists prepackaged with good, as it were, before it comes to our consciousness?

Detmar: It is obvious that knowledge has already been created in a consciousness previously whose purpose is to give our sentience direction and to give us physical presence in an entropically material world; and hence, it was manufactured by a previously existing free will operating within a separate consciousness and whose operations had good about it which was generated by the free will of that consciousness to promote its survival and that of its heirs.

Haskell: Then, this good was previously manufactured and already existed. Therefore, the present free will had nothing to do with it.

Detmar: Well, first, my statement is that all prioritized good is generated by the operation of the free will on the incoming stimuli, or information, to the entity's consciousness, and secondly, even though the good was previously accepted by a predecessor's free will, it is separately existing at the new consciousness and not yet accepted by its free will. Before the good can be totally transferred to the new entity it must be accepted by the new consciousness which means the only way it can become a priority for the new consciousness, is to be accepted by the new entity's free will. That is, the new entity will receive the incoming stimuli which it will note as information - should it be put into memory; there, the free will, which is the rational thinking faculty along with life's energy, or more germane to our discussion, mental effort, will make the decision to accept the incoming information as good for its own purposes.

Haskell: But really, Detmar, is it sometimes a choice? Occasionally, the informational stimuli are so provocative that we cannot resist doing what it intended such as the case for reproduction and all its attendant feelings. We see a beautiful lady and the emotion of desire that develop within us are unbearably strong enough to produce the desired reaction. There is no doubt that much stimuli and information has the intent to, and does, produce a reaction within us. All these feelings come to the consciousness, and our free will many times has little free independent choice but to rubber stamp the original intent that comes with these stimuli. After all, this is the way human beings have many similar traits of behavior as do many species: it is what keeps all species to be the same type of animal. In other words I believe that sometimes the incoming information to the consciousness is so forceful that we are compelled to the information's intended objective.

Detmar: It does not matter whether the incoming informational phenomena has cogency to call a living entity to a specific purpose or whether inanimate circumstances present themselves to a person such as trying to run away from an avalanche if you happen to ski into such a situation or if you get into trouble when swimming and suddenly you find that the rough surf is more than you are physically capable of handling and your free will aptly and without deliberation summarily concludes that you need to vacate your present position and you ski or swim for safety. Or to further the examples, if you come across the one you love and you ask her to commit herself to you, the free will still plays the concluding role, however small, even though the conclusion to the problem is very apparent. It makes the final decision according to its priorities, and this is vital to all of life.

Haskell: Yes. I suppose so. We could say that even in a perilous situation where survival itself is being jeopardized we could choose not to do the obvious and face the consequences, but in almost all cases our desire to survive is overwhelming, and we could say that the free will elects to do the obvious to preserve its survival.

Detmar: The purpose of the free will is to negotiate the circumstances as they arise in its run through life;

to negotiate the risk of being in an entropic universe the anti-entropic entity requires the addition of the free will to meet the perils of the universe and to deal with the various circumstances it meets when in contact with other life entities.

Haskell: It is interesting that in much of the information and knowledge that is inbound to our consciousness we can say that there is intent. Of course, in much of it there is not intent such as when you bump into somebody in a crowd. Here, we receive the information that we have inadvertently touched somebody, but it seems that in such knowledge there seems to be an intention to influence. I would have thought that the purpose of communicative information and knowledge would be ultimately to survive, but it seems there might be a secondary purpose which would be to influence. What do you think, Detmar?

Detmar: You are absolutely right. There is, of course, intent to influence.

Haskell: But even this is not the whole story or the choice of the right words, I think, because even in the inanimate world when one molecule hits another molecule, the one molecule passes influence to another and vice versa. I suppose the difference is that in the inanimate world it is influence without intent whereas in the animate world it is influence with intent.

Detmar: Basically, that is correct. Communication in the animate world is the exporting of stimuli that have the purpose of influence, and the reason for this effort to export influential stimuli is for the purpose of self-survival. All communication by life entities occurs for the purpose of self-preservation. All communication with others is with our own survival in mind, and within that objective its secondary purpose is to take us as far away from misery as possible.

Haskell: I am intrigued that you state that all transference of information is from the perspective of promoting our own survival which I assume includes the survival of the unit family which houses those who will survive us and of promoting our prosperity to take us away from misery.

Detmar: Yes. This is the ultimate purpose of all of life's communication and further within this effort of communication is generally the signal of cooperation. That is, within all social communication the will and intent to cooperation is broadcasted. If it is not social communication, then the factor of volitional cooperation is not imperative.

Haskell: Yes, a thief or robber may communicate that he will take one's goods or money and this may promote his survival, but of course, it does not have the ingredient of cooperation.

Detmar: Yes, and moreover, communication for the purpose of self-survival just by itself is a selfish action and would not necessarily promote mutual, social cooperation. It needs to include the element of cooperation for the purpose of promoting the other's self-survival.

Haskell: Wait. Something is not right here. I understand this need to communicate cooperation in all social situations, otherwise obviously, no one could get along with anybody else, but this added factor of broadcasting the purpose of cooperation to promote the other person's survival is not needed for a social situation which would only need to broadcast the will to cooperate, and the added embellishment that the communication is for the benefit of the other sounds like it is for social and economic situations.

Detmar: That is correct. Just communication is the emission of stimuli from a life entity.

Haskell: Does it not need a receiver to qualify itself

as communication?

Detmar: It does not really matter. Communication only happens when a life entity wants to expend effort for some reason or another but ultimately it can be traced to the purpose of its survival, and due to risk, sometimes - as it is present in any action we do - the attempt does not always come to fruition. But upon our survey of our predicament we try. And in general, we call the attempted thing some name or another, whatever it is (in this case we are calling an attempted action “communication”), even though the attempt may fail. It is just a matter of definition: we may just as well not allow a thing or action to be the recipient of its proper name if it fails. And if we decide that our definition of communication needs a receiver to collect the stimuli, otherwise it would be a failed attempt at communication and therefore not communication and the action not worthy of nomenclatural definition, then we can easily do so.

Haskell: Then, communication is the emission of stimuli along with a sentient receiving of the stimuli.

Detmar: And social communication is the emission of stimuli with the purpose of cooperation, but from now on, since any life entity eschews futile effort, we will presuppose a receptor.

Haskell: Fine.

Detmar: And economic communication is the emission of stimuli with the purpose of cooperation purporting the material benefit of the other or the recipient of the communication.

Haskell: Then the economic communication is of the social communication.

Detmar: Yes. Social communication contains all economic communication.

Haskell: This statement is denoting the difference between social and economic communication, and you specified that the difference is in purporting the benefit of the receiver of the communication. This reminds me of Adam Smith in *The Wealth of Nations* where he advises us that when in commerce we speak not of what will benefit ourselves but what will benefit our partner.

Detmar: Yes. That's absolutely right. We adhere to Adam Smith.

Haskell: But why in communication must there be this purported benefit? Will this lead us to the essence of economics itself and will we be able to realize a separate differentiated equation of economics from the present one? And now that I think of it, does our equation cover social behavior or social decision making?

Detmar: Our equation is the general description of all behavior. When we differentiated out of effort the concept of cooperation, we derived the description of the social situation, and when we again differentiate for production for an expected return, we have the economic equation.

Haskell: Phew! The general description of all behavior!

Detmar: Yes. Decision making is the origin of all behavior. A living entity decides something and then manifests that decision with an action. The general term that covers this is "behavior."

Haskell: Now, I am not so sure any more. For example, previously in our discussion in ethics we came to know that all ethical behavior is that which is of the good. Ethics is the study of the good and bad of behavior. We know that any good action is that which is based in or promotes the survival of the individual and then that of the group. The survival of the individual (and his family) is promoted by socializing with others as we are more efficient as a group than alone. Although there were mountain men, other loners, and ascetics in history that eschewed society, the vehicle by which the promotion, betterment, and proliferation of society and of the human race is achieved is our socializing and this is only done by cooperation which is in our equation. However, we further discussed that the vehicle by which cooperation is effected is through the respect of the individual. We are able to cooperate by our ability to consider the other person which is manifested by respect. When we respect the other person, we are indicating cooperation so that we can socialize and be together for whatever purpose such as just socializing or respecting each other in order to work together to produce something which will further our survival and take us farther away from misery.

Detmar: Correct.

Haskell: Well, we do not have this factor of respect which is the indicator of all good in behavior. Without respect there is no good in behavior and this factor is not in our modular description of decision making.

Detmar: It is within the cooperation factor which differentiates out of the effort factor. We have all the general parameters of behavior, but they are not specific enough to indicate every social situation in particular. By this I mean that the original equations were more general and included all actions even for a lone mountain man of the 19th century who was truly alone and therefore ethics was of no concern. There is no good or bad if you are out of society and alone, and hence, no problems or questions of ethical behavior can arise. However, if we have other people around with whom we decide and need to interact to further our own survival, then we include the factor of cooperation which brings us into society. Within cooperation we can further differentiate out another coefficient of cooperation which would be the concept of respect which allows us to specifically describe every societal action which is of the good, cooperative, productive, and cultural since respect is the manifestation of behavioral culture and the physical culture is demonstrated in the production of goods and services.

Haskell: Yes, I now remember this from our previous session on ethics.

Detmar: As we narrow our behavior we can differentiate out the appropriate factors that will describe all the behavior of that sort. Now, we can know the modular nature of a productive decision or a cultural decision, an ethical decision, a good decision, or more broadly a decision that is not social. The conclusive point here is to indicate that the description is modular and symbolically describable, and as we get more specific in what we would like to denote, the more we differentiate the components and add to the expression with its factors and processes making it more complicated.

Haskell: Let us list them from general to the specific. The final one is, of course, as we already know, composed of effort, risk, time, other subject information, and this together equals a decision which can become a precedent priority. As we already established, we would abbreviate the description as T X R X E X I = the Sacrifice

Detmar: Yes. If we manifest the mental decision with our physical action which is of the effort variable, we get: T X R X E(mental) X I X E(physical) = The Sacrifice X E(physical) which would be Time X Risk X Effort squared times Information which would equal the Reward which is a good or a service. But as you pointed out, within our effort there is cooperation and within cooperation there is respect. And hence, if we were to quantify those ingredients and include them specifically in our modular expression of behavior, we could say the following: any other relevant Information X Time X Risk X Respectful Effort, which is a function of Cooperative Effort which is a function of our will to employ our effort, equals the Reward, or that is, the goods or services that are the result of the decisions.

Haskell: I somewhat see.

Detmar: The original modular expression gives us the Sacrifice. This employs only mental effort and the result is noted as the sacrifice that would be required if a physical action were employed. This is the broadest expression of life's behavior. The second state is the description of the actual physical reward (or service) that is a result of employing physical action. The physical action begets a physical reward.

Haskell: OK.

Detmar: In further differentiating the modular behavioral equation, either the mental or physical sacrifice, we can become more specific should we find factors that are always present when we want to describe more specific behaviors such as the will or the physical behavior to cooperate to obtain a reward that requires a societal situation such as when we want to produce something complex and we need to cooperate with others to obtain it.

Haskell: I see. He differentiates the need to cooperate out of the effort factor because in every case in order to work with others we need to cooperate, and in the expression we can note effort as a function of our will to cooperate. If we employ physical effort, we will obtain (most likely, although sometimes not, depending on the risk factor) the reward.

Detmar: Right. If we further differentiate the cooperation, we can further make our expression to include respect because the vehicle by which we are able to cooperate is respect; and hence, in every cooperative situation one will find respect. Respectful behavior allows us to cooperate in order for us to produce for our family, to survive, and get us as far away from misery as possible. Hence, if respect is an integral part of all cooperation, then it should be included in the equational expression of that which is compensatory of our mental sacrifice first and integrative on physical efforts.

Haskell: You say "integrative."

Detmar: Yes. We are essentially using the process of integration when we go from the mental general expression of behavior that is the Sacrifice to the use of physical effort that generates the physical productive results, or the Reward.

Chapter Three - Economic Behavior

Haskell: Well, Detmar, you indicate that we essentially have a modular expression of the production of something which is the same thing as saying that we have parsed the nature of economics, since that which is productive - it would seem to me - would be of the economic. From this we could determine a definition of economics, and it seems that it may be different from the classical one. But first, let's go back to my previously iterated interrogative about the asseveration of economic communication holding the requirement of interest in the other person's benefit.

Detmar: Yes. The communicative stage of the economic behavior expression seeks the reward of confirmation of the other's interest that is common to the originator's interest. At the communicative stage the product is the intelligence of benefit and the reward is the same.

Haskell: I do not follow you.

Detmar: In the basic non-social situation we have information come to us that we set against a priority such as the determination that we should go across the street to the ice cream shop and allay our sudden craving for ice cream. It requires no one else and no cooperation and therefore no communication to set up the cooperation.

Haskell: Correct.

Detmar: However, in order to describe the social situation we differentiate the effort variable to include the factor of cooperation. Preparatory to cooperation within the factor of effort we need to communicate our willingness to cooperate and within this willingness there is the communicative need to export our will to address the needs of those with whom we will cooperate. After all, the essence of cooperation is the consideration of the other.

Haskell: Yes, I understand as I recall our disquisition in ethics and am integrating that understanding into the present topic of social economic behavior. To summarize, the manifestation of respect is due to the degree of consideration of the other with whom we cooperate. The more we consider someone, the more we respect that person due to our need or desire to cooperate with him. If we consider them extremely important to our purposes of survival and happiness, then we respect them in whatever way we are considering them. If the consideration of them is financially oriented, our respect will appear socially and monetarily, and the consideration will take the form of money as well as a social manifestation of respect such as the hand shake and polite speaking. The expression "in consideration of" one dollar indicates that we respect another individual in that he produces something that we value to the extent of one dollar and we respect him accordingly, at least to the extent of one dollar, monetarily speaking. Of course, socially speaking, we may or may not respect the individual as we consider him a friend or not as a friend.

Detmar: Correct. We discussed these aspects of ethics extensively in our previous interview.

Haskell: So, as I understand it, we must communicate the consideration of the other whether it be in a social situation when we communicate that we want to develop friendship by our consideration of the social partner indicated by our socially respectful language, or in an economic situation when we communicate our commercial consideration of the other party many times enumerated by the signal of how much we will pay monetarily for something or by indicating how much something that we have or will produce costs. In a barter situation the consideration is in the production of goods or services and in an advanced economy the consideration of the other will be communicated in financial instruments. Hence, to initiate cooperation we need to communicate our willingness to consider the other.

Detmar: Yes.

Haskell: Then the economic expression should be Pertinent Information X Time X (Mental Effort x Physical Effort x Cooperative Effort (usually in the form of monetary consideration)) X Risk = The Economic Reward.

Detmar: Yes. In abbreviated form we could say:

I X R X T X E3 = The Economic Reward

That is, we have integrated from the Sacrifice to the Economic Reward by multiplying both sides of the expression Physical Effort times Cooperative Considerative Effort. Hence,

R X T X I X E X E2 = The Sacrifice X E2 = The Economic Reward

Haskell: Then, is this equational expression indicative of the economic transaction?

Detmar: Yes.

Haskell: How so? A transaction indicates a quid pro quo.

Detmar: It is an equation and both sides will be the same conceptually; and quantitatively, they will strive to be the same although this does not always happen due to risk and the diligence (a kind of effort) by each side. But if there are two parties, then both sides of the equation will be the same indicating a single transaction between two parties which one side may be called the economic sacrifice and the other side is the economic reward. Hence, I X T X R X E3 (which is the Sacrifice of one party) = The Economic Reward = I X T X R X E3 (the Economic Sacrifice of the second party).

Haskell: Well, if this is so, we may delve into some interesting subjects in which I have a keen interest. Let us start by asking if we can determine, by what we have established so far, that our equation is correlational to the classic definition of economics which is the study of the distribution of limited resources or one that I would like to suggest which is the study of supply and demand.

Detmar: Economics is, more precisely, the study of production.

Haskell: Really? What happened to supply and demand or the use of limited resources?

Detmar: This new definition adheres closely to the modular expression we have derived. More precisely, economics is the study of the time, effort and resources we expend amidst an atmosphere of risk in order to effect production that will promote our survival and take us way from misery.

Haskell: What about the other side of the coin? What about demand?

Detmar: Economics does not need to study demand because demand is inherent in our desire to survive and bring ourselves up and away from misery. It is an already established priority previous to the advent of any production. Therefore, the discipline of economics does not technically include demand as a component for study: it is a prerequisite for production and hence for the study of economics. If there were not this innate natural existence for the need for production to take us away from misery and base subsistence, there would be no production.

Haskell: I am not sure I quite understand this.

Detmar: All demand is pre-existing knowledge derived as priorities known here in its general form as a reward, or potential reward, and our working to obtain the reward is the sacrifice.

Haskell: I see.

Detmar: Our priorities are how we want to run our life in the short and long term and the yardstick by which we prioritize is basically that which promotes our survival and takes us as far away from misery as possible.

Haskell: And that which is very basic to our survival on a daily basis would get high priority and that which is farther away from our basic needs such as a dessert would get a little less priority and those things that are considered a luxury would get even less.

Detmar: Precisely. As we are able to cover and provide for the basic needs, the position of the priority will move farther up the scale away from the necessities and more toward pleasure and luxury.

Haskell: Well, that reminds me about something you said earlier. You mentioned, that all actions that we do, originate in our need to survive. I am not sure I can agree with this because once we get into the area of acquiring luxury items and doing things for the fun of it, it does not seem that these things originate in survival. For example, just the action of sitting down and playing a game of chess or talking with friends over a beer or going on vacation or anything we do just for the pleasure of it does not seem to be action that is based in survival. It is not for sure that any action that we may do for the purpose of pleasure or fun is based in the promotion of our existence but something beyond that. It does not seem to me that all actions are based in survival.

Detmar: Not directly anyway, but ultimately, yes. Everything we do is ultimately steeped in survival.

Haskell: Well, please start with explaining my example of our decisions to have fun or enjoy something pleasurable. Perhaps I should ask what is the purpose of pleasure and why should we even be able to experience it.

Detmar: We need pleasure to enable us to know which and what things are good for us and would take us away from bare existence and misery to a better life that promotes our overall well-being. The ability to know and experience pleasure and fun gives us direction and points us in the right direction away from death, degradation, bare subsistence, probable extinction and improbable completion of our requisite mandate to reproduce, proliferate, and populate the earth with life.

Haskell: What? Have we such a clear purposeful mandate and is it that just this specific knowledge of what is pleasurable is an important cog in this mandate?

Detmar: Absolutely. As we discussed in our last interview on truth and free will and as you noted in your published notes of that transcription, knowledge had to be present when the first molecules went from an entropic condition to anti-entropic life possessive as it takes knowledge to be anti-entropic since the molecules have to make decisions and know what to do. Hence, at the inception of life, knowledge was present and this knowledge had to pre-exist because the second law of thermodynamics prevents the entropic condition of matter from manufacturing or retaining knowledge or anything else. Consequently, life was purposely conceived and purpose indicates design and objective, and in combination with life we can conclude that within that purpose there is the objective for design of that which is good for life thus making it an absolute value and this understanding is within all of life's entities.

Haskell: Yes. I remember now.

Detmar: And the nature of this good is that which promotes life itself: those actions that promote the well-being of the life entity and its progeny first is mandated goodness; and should the individuals be necessarily societal, which by the way will be a goodness in itselfbecause societal species congregate cooperatively for no other reason than to promote the survival of the species and the individuals therein, then those actions that promote the society will be of the good.

Haskell: But what about the existence of what seems to be unadulterated pleasure where there seems to be no productive good to qualify it within the scope of goodness. Pleasure and fun seem to be outside this realm of absolute values for life that hold this idea of that which promotes the survival of life is good. It seems that which we associate with what is good for life's entities, or specifically that which would promote man's survival, may not be totally reconcilable in that it is clear that shear pleasure leads to what we might call hedonistic, materialistic, or degradative behavior.

Detmar: The sense of pleasure is surely needed just as is the sensation of pain. We need to know when something is bad for us and pain delivers this information immediately and efficiently.

Haskell: I should say so.

Detmar: It is not enough that our intellect applies itself to every problem of existence and sorts out each predicament. Our thought processes would not keep us alive very long should we not have the ability to feel pain. With each problem we would have to intellectually decipher the occurring problem, and when something should go wrong with us, such as when we undergo an accident of some sort and incur a bodily injury, without an indication of pain from our senses, we may not even be able to recognize that something is wrong with us. And even if we can know by cerebral means alone, most likely we will not be able to know the intensity of the problem.

Haskell: Yes. I do not disagree about the sense of pain. It is clear that we need this sense, unfortunately, in order to live: the nervous system is vital with all its functions, to say the least. It is in the opposite direction that I make my inquiry.

Detmar: In the reverse fashion we need to have our sense of pleasure to know which direction to point ourselves. This sense helps us direct ourselves in the direction away from misery. We have discussed previously in other interlocutions that inherent in our modus operandi, as life entities, we are imbued with the purpose of existence and the will to live and survive, and that the essence of what is good is that which promotes survival for us and takes us away from misery and that the senses of pleasure and pain are the engines which help us decide in what direction we should go in our lives. Of course, the intellect harbored within our free will is important also to help us discern the solution to the complicated problems of existence, but even there, the intellect uses the yard-stick of pleasure to help make its choices in guiding us through our daily predicaments. The existence of pleasure and pain is a direct consequence of being sentient in an existence which has risk and where decisions are requisite.

Haskell: OK. It seems that pleasure would be helpful in establishing the direction that we should take in living our lives as it would facilitate the efficacious decisions that will promote our survival and take us away from misery. However, it is the problem of too much pleasure that concerns me; it seems that just the feeling of fun and sheer pleasure holds no advantages to our survival. It appears that there can be too much enjoyment; pleasure and fun that has no worth to us generically exist, and I would call this situation materialistic or hedonistic. To this problem would you be able to proffer a definition to help me understand these concepts so that maybe we can know when pleasure is good and when or how it becomes too much or too intense and no longer directive of our overall survival and well-being?

Detmar: Surely. Materialism is the incremental addition of things to our possessions that has no additional value for our survival and does not take us away from misery.

Haskell: And hedonism?

Detmar: Hedonism is the incremental increase of pleasure that has no directional value for our survival and does not incrementally take us any further away from misery.

Haskell: Could you explain this a bit more fully? How is it we can say that someone is materialistic or that person is hedonistic?

Detmar: Even though our definition is concrete, understandable, and clearly limned, to denote whether someone is materialistic or hedonistic is difficult, but through the additional use of our aesthetic sense, we can make our decisions.

Haskell: How so?

Detmar: As economists explain, all things are produced for the ultimate consumption at the consumer level and this is applicable for all life. Life uses its time and expends its effort amidst a world of risk to produce things that will promote its existence, and if possible, life's entities would like to produce enough so that it could enjoy some pleasure. This indicates that there exists a margin between its predicament and bare subsistence.

Haskell: So far, so good, as this has already been established.

Detmar: As we produce to administer to our needs, we experience pleasure, as misery is banished, and this feeling of pleasure indicates that we are doing the right thing for our unit family and ourselves. We continue to produce because there is an innate want to satisfy our feeling to go away from misery and satisfy our wants. This is pleasurable, and hence, we continually come up with additional items to fill this ongoing directional life force of pleasure. Initially, as things are produced to fulfill our basic needs, we make large quantum leaps in the fulfillment of pleasure which is clearly of the good such as farming which produces food, building schools to teach our progeny, the manufacture of transportation vehicles to take us to places of production. The list is endless, each item fulfilling an appropriate niche in the ongoing engine of survival and hopefully advancing survival away from misery upward toward pleasure.

Haskell: I am following you and agree with most everything (except for maybe your nebulous statement concerning demand) so far.

Detmar: As production fulfills the basic needs and advances toward the less needed, but nevertheless pleasurable, the absolute need, or that is, the prioritization of the production, goes down, exempli gratia, food and clothes are prioritized before a luxury condominium at our favorite ski resort. As the priority diminishes (yet the pleasure remains constant), the danger of materialism appears because at some point the benefit of the added consumable production diminishes to a negligible amount and the pleasure for the most part also diminishes compared to earlier and greater prioritizations. When we reach this point where the added consumable production that we receive lends little, none, or even a negative increment, materialism appears, and in the case of the added increment being a tactile pleasure as opposed to tangible production, hedonism appears.

Haskell: Do you have any examples? How about a collector? Is he materialistic?

Detmar: Possibly, but probably not. Let's say we are collectors of pocket watches. First, we know the value of a watch and that it is an important machine. Along with its purpose it has a history both in its use and in the design that artisans have embroidered on them. Through our aesthetic sense, we enjoy this craftsmanship that has created their beauty. Naturally, with the first one we acquire, we are very appreciative of its use and beauty. Hopefully, we either display it or wear it. Acquiring a second one might be used for formal occasions or any other secondary purpose. However, as we acquire more, sooner or later a redundancy, at least, for use will occur, and hence, the danger of materialism arises.

Haskell: OK.

Detmar: It may arise because the total net effect of the additional acquisition will have a negative effect

- or it may not. If our aesthetic sense is fully satisfied and we display the watch so that we may view its artisan's artistic beauty, then perhaps it allows us significant aesthetic pleasure and we skirt the problem of materialism. However, if it does not give us that extra enjoyment and pleasure of the aesthetic and we store the beautiful watch never to have use of a view of it for its aesthetic value, we cross the line into materialism because of the lack of aesthetic or otherwise positive enjoyment in it, and it does not take us any further away from misery.

Haskell: And I suppose in the same way in the case of physical enjoyment, that should we enjoy the act of eating and that should we eat in excess to the extent that the extra eating does not deliver much if at all any additional culinary delight but the deleterious (and hence, there appears a total incremental negative effect), we may conclude that we have become hedonistic in this regard to this particular extent.

Detmar: Yes.

Haskell: Well, before this subject of the purpose of pleasure we were speaking of the pre-existence of demand to production - that in order for production to exist there is the built-in motivation for needs and a demand to live better and the desire to divorce ourselves from the trials of hard living and to survive in an easier fashion. Everybody wants to be comfortable and strive to improve their condition.

Detmar: Yes, naturally.

Haskell: And that the study of economics is the science of production which leads me to wonder about the old question of whether economics is a social (and therefore inexact) science or a natural science.

Detmar: It is a social science wrapped within a natural science. It is the study of production, and its modularity, as being described here by us, is, prima facie, demonstrably a natural science. However, within this natural science is the component of effort with its coefficient of cooperation, and because of the existence of cooperation within the framework of the natural science, the presence of a social science appears as the concept of "social" necessarily presupposes the existence of cooperation which allows us to be social.

Haskell: I see. Well, let's go over some of the terms that appear in the science of economics and see where they exist within our modular statement of the science of production.

Detmar: Economics is more precisely the nature of the production equation. The economic decision expressed is the equation equaling the Reward which is produced.

Haskell: How would we denote any of the common economic terms such as growth, investment, supply and demand, profit, and capital? I should point out that in our equational expression that would cover the economic situation there is an apparent deficiency: it should indicate the existence of capital for it is clear that in order to obtain any economic reward, capital and labor would be required to adequately complete the expression, and we have only noted labor which I assume could be derived from Effort which is already expressed.

Detmar: Excellent observation, Haskell. Capital, as well as labor, is differentiated out of effort. But let us make a few distinctions within this concept of "capital." First, capital is anything that we possess including our labor and our natural resources. Capital goods would be anything that we produce including that which has already been produced and passed on in exchange for other capital goods or for promissory notes to the right to purchase goods and services in the future, which is also known as money, or anything that represents production of goods or services - even gold can be a note indicating former production and therefore possessing the power to purchase. Without production of something, there can be no money; or more precisely, money can have no value.

Haskell: But capital seems to me to be quite separate from labor as capital is material, and labor is effort-action which is energy related, and I believe a college text in economics would agree.

Detmar: The original purpose of all capital is to increase the efficiency of effort. Effort, or labor, and free will were first required to obtain the original capital. When man first created a capital object such as a tool which enabled him to more efficiently produce a desired reward, he used free will along with effort to create the tool. The primitive inventor, allowing his creative free will to decide that he should employ a straight piece of wood with a sharp end to promote the effectuation of the hunting of animal meat, made the effort to search for suitable wood, found a sharp stone to make the end pointed, and produced an arrow, a spear or whatever tool or machine; to wit, some sort of scenario depicting the making of the tool from his effort must have occurred. This tool, now a capital object, will make our enterprising hunter more efficient in obtaining animal meat which will promote his survival and take him farther away from misery by providing for himself and his unit family with more meat to consume.

Haskell: I see. And from this original effort to make the first capital good we can envision the proliferation of goods and services as the combination of free will, information, effort, and capital recombine to generate more goods and services. I read an excellent exposition on how the history of information and knowledge precipitated the expansion of capital goods and the efficiency of services, called *Bionomics* by Michael Rothschild.

Detmar: An excellent monograph.

Haskell: But still, how do we incorporate capital into our equational expression?

Detmar: As free will operates upon the variables of the equation, we can know that capital is differentiated out of effort and hence:

Risk X Information X Time X Effort(Mental) x Effort (Physical) = The Sacrifice (Mental) X Effort (Physical) = The Sacrifice (Mental-Physical) = The Reward (or Interim Reward)

And the Reward in this case due to the

sagacity and ingenuity of the free will operating with the information and knowledge factor is an interim reward but nevertheless a reward in of itself. If we take this interim reward, which is a capital good, and recombine it with the equation by multiplying both sides of the equation again, we will get:

(R)(I)(T)(E2) X Interim Reward (Capital) =
Reward X Interim Reward (Capital) = Final Reward (Consumer Good),

and to abbreviate this, we get letting C = Interim Reward (Capital):

(R)(I)(T)(E2C) = Consumer Good

Of course, there may be any number of interim steps of capital good production thereby causing the numerical exponential of our Capital variable to increase, or for that matter any of the variables can be increased as needed in the process depending on the complexity of production and how many times we reconsider the individual variables in the expression in the production of the final good or service.

Haskell: But still, I have to object because capital is a material thing and we have not described capital in any way material. In order for our equation to be consistent with dimensional analysis, it certainly seems to me that the equation that describes the Reward should include a dimension of mass in its description.

Detmar: It may or may not.

Haskell: Well, let us first define capital.

Detmar: Capital is any instrument that facilitates production, and it can be either effort or physically related.

Haskell: So, it could have a physical parameter and hence, a material dimension?

Detmar: Of course. It depends on our existential position of reference that we spoke about in our last interview.

Haskell: What are you talking about?

Detmar: The purpose of capital is to make production more efficient; it is labor saving and even labor enabling whereby we can do things now with machines that we could not do just by our hands.

Haskell: Of course.

Detmar: So, the purpose is entirely to augment our efforts making them easier, more efficient, and enabling us to do and produce more.

Haskell: I agree.

Detmar: The essence of capital can be either energy or matter, and they are ultimately interchangeable, or so, the physicists tell us. And when the reward that we seek is physical, the dimensional analysis should have a mass denoting parameter. When it is entirely within the service sector, it will not have one.

Haskell: OK, I agree.

Detmar: As we discussed when the first tool - the first capital item - was invented, it was produced through a decision involving time, risk, knowledge, and effort. The result of the decision was an application of physical effort added to both sides of the equation through multiplication giving us a capital item.

Haskell: So?

Detmar: From the effort we got the capital item without the addition of the mass factor to the equation. The first tool was constructed through knowledge which came forth through the creative function of our free will.

Haskell: This seems significant, but why, I do not know.

Detmar: It is because through our decision to apply physical effort we have effected the production of something. The first tool, let's say it was a sharp rock, was the interim capital object that was used to effect a pointed object that could be used for hunting, making the early hominid more effective in acquiring meat for himself and family. His physical actions produced the machine which produced the reward.

Haskell: As I am iterating.

Detmar: But the reward is actually in the frame of relevancy of the equation for the quelling of the pangs of hunger which is a form of information coming to the arena of our consciousness from the ingesting of the meat. Our energy produces a sensation, or anti-sensation, at the consciousness. Our frame of relevancy is at the level of the decision maker in his consciousness and the reward is also there: when the physical object of the meat arrives, is cooked, deposited in the mouth, ingested, and mitigates the feelings of the hunger which comes to the sentient palate in the complex arena of the myriad of sensations, the particular sensation of hunger is mollified and quelled.

Haskell: I think I understand. If we decided to add mass to the capital object to the equation, then we will receive in return the physical reward. As it is now, the effort without the mass begets the energy of the food - the reward also, but at the non-physical level - to quell our feelings of hunger which is the priority that leads us to the decision to seek and obtain the energy of the food.

Detmar: Right.

Haskell: And so, adding to both sides of the equation the effect of the effort applied to the bio-mass will obtain the dimensional consistency that we seek.

Detmar: Yes.

Haskell: And perhaps, we could call it the physical effort and just give it the added component of mass that I seek. After all, physical endeavor, it seems to me, would be effort plus the actual physical life that allows us to effectuate our wishes in this corporeal world.

Detmar: It sounds good to me; and this allows us to realize that the essence of a capital reward is knowledge, mass-effort, time, and a probability.

Haskell: Yes, I agree. Every capital object involves clearly a mass, time in its making, an effort and know-how to create it.

Detmar: Good.

Haskell: OK. Let's return to our subject of economics; what about the other factors of economic statements such as growth or investment? How do we incorporate these concepts into our equation which will allow us to get something close to what actually occurs in commerce?

Detmar: All growth is derived from an increase of production which is achieved by adding another person to the economy (which would mean another equation) who starts to do or make something, or is achieved by the individual manufacturer or provider of a service to expand his output by either increasing one or more of the individual factors noted in the equational expression. He either tries harder intensifying his effort, or he employs his free will in combination with information to create new knowledge that will allow him to become more efficient. This will enable him to use less time or decrease his risk to permit him to diminish his effort and still produce as much by the use of a capital good as the capital good is a derivative of the effort factor in combination with his free will. A capital good is mechanical effort created from our rationalities and knowledge usually applied to a physical thing: and a service - or that is, a capital service - is the rationality and knowledge applied to our physical effort, or labor.

Haskell: I think I see. We must act upon one of the factors in the equational expression to cause its resultant effect to become more efficient in the Economic Sacrifice, or that is, the Reward.

Detmar: There must be an inertia set up to act upon one or more of the factors.

Haskell: OK. Let's go over them one at a time.

Detmar: The risk factor can be decreased in a number of ways such as changing geographic locations or choosing the people you deal with or by eating better food and developing better medicines to make us healthier and thereby decreasing the risk of ill health.

Haskell: But the one factor depends on other factors

such as effort to decrease the risk which is the result and not a factor.

Detmar: That really does not matter. It is a factor in the Sacrifice. Of course, we need to keep the risk of any situation diminished to help ensure the success of the Sacrifice, and we decrease this risk by the method employed in any decision as we have already delineated. If risk in a particular situation is a problem as it runs up against a priority, we conclude from the establishment of the previous priority that we need to reduce the risk. We act upon this by employing the other factors of the equation which would be time, information, and effort (and its derivatives of cooperation and capital) as acted upon by the free will. If we are at the thought level of the decision, the result is a mental sacrifice; if we are at the action level of the decision, then the result is the Mental-Physical Reward.

Haskell: I see. If we perceive the risk is high in a certain situation, we set up the decisional equation with the sacrifice being the necessary diminution of the risk in the situation as it is perceived that the risk exceeds our priority that is set for that situation. And from the decision an action is set in motion to ameliorate the risk in accordance with the priority, and the action - or actions - may take many forms as already suggested.

Detmar: Correct.

Haskell: Once the risk is reduced to an acceptable level, we can proceed with the Reward that we have decided to obtain.

Detmar: The same method is applied for time. If the Reward will take too long to obtain as set against a previously established priority, then we decide to either not proceed with the obtainment of the Reward or we conclude that the time must be lessened.

Haskell: How do we come to this conclusion that the time must be shortened or the risk diminished? I think we have gone over this, but let us do it again for clarity sake.

Detmar: Information comes to our consciousness creating a situation where a decision is needed as a previously established priority demands.

Haskell: Yes. Situations abound in our daily lives: we could realize we are sick and it is a priority that we want to get well; we are hungry and we want, naturally, to alleviate the pangs of hunger; we want to sleep or meet our friends or whatever.

Detmar: There is a desideratum - a priority - and in order to obtain this object (a material good) or action (a service) we decide it first at the mental level, which we will call "The Sacrifice," and this decision is denoted as Time X Information X Risk X Mental Effort with our free will as the determinator of the quantities that we perceive, and with these quantities we calculate the equation, and then see how this compares to the priority that created the situation.

Haskell: I remember. Taking as an example the situation of planting a vegetable garden, we perceive and know that we get hungry and have established previously that we want to avoid hunger.

Detmar: Yes. Let me point out here that whatever example you choose, it can range from a very basic priority, exempli gratia, the satisfaction of immediate hunger or the priority of becoming well if we are sick, to a complicated example of what car to buy or what career to choose or what book to buy or with which friends to socialize. These are complicated situations because they are far from basic subsistence and happen when there is a little pleasure in our lives and we have the luxury of their occurrence. We are glad to have these decisions as they are layered on top of many previous mean subsistence decisions that have thankfully already become previously established priorities and do not need to be attended to. When we are sick in bed, we deal only with the priority of getting well and not much else matters as the priority is of the base subsistent level and all consuming. To this bare situation we have attached the high priority of getting well because it means just surviving which is all important. Without getting past this priority the others farther along the scale such as which car to buy has no relevance to our situation and does not matter at all. In dealing with the sickness we have the priority to get well again and our free will calculates whether the attainment of the highly prioritized desideratum of getting well is worth it, and in this case because the priority is high, the score of our calculative equation easily reaches the priority, and the free will initiates the action to consummate the Reward of the calculative expression of allowing us to expend the effort, take the time, and use know-how such as using the available medicine in a secure place, such as a bed, in order to get well.

Haskell: I see. So, in a more complicated or layered situation when we are not so close to just surviving but are away from misery or base subsistence such as in buying a car, we establish the priority of the car, and we estimate the amount of effort and capital that would be needed, the time it requires, any risk involved, and use the information available such as how to do it and calculate: the calculations will then tell us whether we can go and to which automobile dealership to buy which type of car.

Detmar: Precisely.

Chapter 4 - Quantifying Economic Concepts

Haskell: Then, let us get back to the problem of economic growth.

Detmar: Sure.

Haskell: You mentioned that if we add effort, there will be growth. I was thinking that adding labor is the same as adding effort, and in recent literature there is the topic of what fuels growth and whether sometimes when there is an addition to the labor force there may not be growth - but a negative growth per capita may occur - as the economy becomes burdened with this extra labor force which will drive the price (or value) of labor (or effort) down indicating that there is no growth per capita, that is, there is no growth commensurate with this labor influx. There are more people to be supported by the same production, or perhaps, there is an disproportionately small incremental increase due to the lower labor cost which allows the cost of production to go down, thereby, the demand may increase. Some conjecture that just an overall increase of labor to any economy will bring the standard of living down. Probably, a good example of this argument is why a country should keep its borders closed to open immigration and only allow controlled growth of labor.

Detmar: Yes, I have occasionally read of some essays of this concern.

H; And this problem assumes that our equational expression is for all economic entities - individual or corporate.

Detmar: Yes, of course. As long as it is a life entity, our calculative equation applies. All life operates along the same principles of decision making; it is just that although the very basic priorities of the will to survive, reproduce, avoid pain, keep away from misery, avoid hunger, and the such are the same, the complicated, advanced priorities change. And if the same species with the same general priorities band together to make decisions en masse, they will use the same collective process as the individual to finalize its decision.

Haskell: OK. But getting back to the economic decision of open immigration, we must first consider another problem before this one. We know that if there is this problem of a company having the opportunity of choosing between cheap labor and expensive labor which has the same output, the company will surely select the least expensive because its production of goods becomes less costly, and it can be said that its production becomes more efficient, and it wants to become more efficient because of fear of its competitors and of its desire to increase profits.

Detmar: Yes.

Haskell: Well, it seems that this is a priority that pervades all economic choices and should be included in the equation. Also, it seems to be a priority that is not decisional. That is, we had no need to decide this; it is obvious to anyone without thinking about it, without making a decision, that efficiency is a natural priority for any economic decision to be based. I believe that we base all economic decisions on efficiency.

Detmar: Excellent point. And yes, efficiency is a priority, and it is a basic one. Upon a cursory glance we do not discern that it is a priority constructed in the same manner as all the others. But because it is a foundational priority, we begin to realize it very early in our construction of priorities, and we understand it to be innate, natural, or God given if you will.

Haskell: I do not understand.

Detmar: If in any situation there is a choice and a decision is made, then there are priorities involved and ones that were previously established all the way back to the original ones - the most basic one being that of survival. We make a choice of surviving and confirm this choice on a daily basis when we arise each morning, and it is usually an easy one. We arise, and in our arena of consciousness we take in the day's immediate information to make this confirmation of survival. We do not have overriding pain, things are tolerable, and we have pleasure in our lives. We fill in the slots in our equation, set it against our priority of survival, and we note that we should continue with survival. The time slot is not a factor because we are existing and we enjoy the passing of time; the risk of survival is low because we feel we will most probably be able to get through the day without any overwhelming pain and tragedy befalling us; the effort to survive is not a burden but probably actually pleasant to experience and the information-stimuli that comes to our consciousness looks like it is an overall positive experience.

Haskell: I see.

Detmar: Only three things are outside our ken of choice: first is the fact that we have come into existence as we experience our free will (Descartes would say that we think), and secondly, that there is incoming stimuli to our consciousness. As for these two matters we have no choice available: as we exist, we will experience.

Haskell: A little twist on Descartes' famous statement.

Detmar: As these two factors have no choice about them, they are not priorities, they are absolute conditions to our predicament. Also, within the incoming stimuli to our arena of the consciousness there are types of experiences that seem irrepressible, constant, and attentively demanding.

Haskell: You are referring here to innate desires, feelings, and thoughts that we all have which we would call genetic, biological or environmentally induced behavior.

Detmar: Correct.

Haskell: But if it is innate and biologically induced, the choice is not ours, but that of our antecedents, biologically, and ultimately induced by our heavenly father.

Detmar: The information stimuli coming to the consciousness can be overwhelmingly slanted to induce certain behavior, but the free will has last right of refusal to take a different course should circumstances arise that alter the decisional equation. The life entity needs to be versatile amidst the miasma of risk. We are programmed to react in certain ways to certain incoming informational stimuli, but life must be ready to change and recognize the need should additional information indicate the new situation.

Haskell: The problem that remains in my mind is that in your explanation of the system of our decisional process set against our priorities it seems that we have very little innate behavior, that we are programmed very little and everything is controlled by the logic abounding in the free will in the arena of the consciousness, and I believe from my readings in genetics and other writings in behavioral biology that there is much genetically induced behavior and there is very little we can do about it.

Detmar: That's right. This behavior ranges from that about which we can do nothing which are absolutes for our consciousness, examples of which are the realizations that we exist and that there are incoming stimuli to our consciousness, to things that we have only a little control over, such as, our response to the sight of a beautiful women or the aesthetic pleasure of a magnificent view or the satisfaction of the palette as we experience culinary delight to something we have total control over such as the choice of what kind of car we would like to buy. This degree of the freedom of the free will of the consciousness to decide correlates exactly with the degree and intensity of the system of priorities that our consciousness recognizes as set up by the free will in reaction to the incoming informational stimuli.

Haskell: It is this point where we move from the absolute to the arrival of the free will to order our lives that interests me; something is not complete in my understanding. Even though we have a choice, it really seems that we do not have a choice. I do not know what to ask here.

Detmar: To complete the picture, we must add another absolute to our situation. When the incoming informational stimuli arrive at the consciousness, there is a necessary response of pleasure or pain and this takes us into a transition and for the need of the free will.

Haskell: I am listening.

Detmar: The cause and effect relationship in the arena of the consciousness is an absolute for our existence. We have the situation of our existence, the informational stimuli pinging on our consciousness unstoppably, and also have the undeniable response of pleasure or pain. Our consciousness uses this response of pleasure to gage its selection of the priority of its action. The initial selections of priorities become primary to our foundation of behavior such as to continue to exist. At the level of the consciousness we are informed that we exist, and the response to this is that this is either pleasurable or painful. These happenings are absolute for any life entity in that we cannot avoid it if we are living. But at this point because of the nature of our environment we are subject to chance as things change constantly, and hence, the incoming stimuli to the consciousness varies and accordingly so does our response of either pleasure or pain. At this point our free will steps in to modulate the mixture and direct the life entity to keep its operation heading toward the pleasure side of the ledger. As our situation develops and our life becomes complicated, the decisions sometimes become correspondingly convoluted in keeping us on the pleasurable tract.

Haskell: Yes. I am beginning to understand. And our decisions to head us toward pleasure away from pain and misery are the precedent priorities that we establish for ourselves and our decisional equation is the method that we employ in our consciousness to effect the best course for us.

Detmar: Correct.

Haskell: But what about many of the emotions that are not of pleasure or pain such as anger, hate, admiration, revenge, or allegiance, and many others?

Detmar: All emotions are derivatives of pleasure or pain just as cooperation is a derivative of effort which can be either of pain or pleasure depending on whether we are undergoing an unwilling sacrifice or a willing one. Hence, anger and hate are not of pleasure (unless it is deviant behavior); it is not a pleasure to be angry at people; when we are, we are not in a good mood, and we are not happy, and it is the unpleasant situation that produces the anger in us.

Haskell: Admiration would be of the pleasure directive as we would have a good feeling for someone. This seems to fit how I see and experience things. Let's get back to my concern about the decisional model of the priority of efficiency since it is a very basic one although it still seems to me to be an absolute for life entities.

Detmar: Efficiency is not an absolute because we have a choice. The free will can decide if there are pressing circumstances to not choose the efficient route. But because the equational expression calculates it giving it a high score, efficiency becomes a basic priority.

Haskell: Alright.

Detmar: Regarding the subject of directive behavior that is innate and genetically induced, these interior originating experiences that come to our consciousness inform us that there is pleasure whether cerebral or physical, and our free will calculates the cost of following these directives double checking to make sure that the adherence to these mandates is commensurate with our present predicament. If the calculation of the information indicates that the cost of following these desires is low, the free will clears the way for our compliance.

Haskell: So, there is innate behavior that induces us to follow what it wants, but we only do so upon the free will's checking the situation and confirming whether it is agreeable or not.

Detmar: Yes.

Haskell: But we make so many mistakes. Perhaps our free will or the equation we use is faulty.

Detmar: Well, you bet we make mistakes, and it is for a variety of reasons: there is the presence of risk for which we cannot prepare adequately and perfectly; there are the limitations of our free will which is composed of effort and our mental faculties that cannot calculate everything and its powers of perception are limited; all the information in each situation may not reach our consciousness; or there may not be time enough for the free will to come to its proper conclusion. It is a chaotic universe with rapidly changing situations and all calculations have to deal with this chaos and risk.

Haskell: Yes, one's judgment is only as good as one's knowledge. Well, I think we can finally get back to the question of economic growth, labor, the effort of our equation, and the problem of immigration. How can we find a solution to this well known issue?

Detmar: As we mentioned, effort is one of the ingredients of our equation and adding more to the labor factor will change the result of our equation, and therefore, we can know that we will have growth. We can add to the effort factor by increasing the number of man-hours if we have an influx of labor or an increase in the intensity of the man-hours (should a single man work harder and more efficiently).

Haskell: And naturally, this is preferable to anybody who would want to increase his production by making his situation more efficient as noted by our priority to do so. But if a manufacturer were to replace one worker with a new arrival that is willing to work at a lesser wage, what are the ramifications? Because of the new arrival, there is an increase to the general population, and whoever gets the job at the factory it will be at the new lesser competitive wage. Overall, is this good or is it bad to see the new arrivals into the work force driving down the wage but making the manufacturer more efficient?

Detmar: Actually, we should not look at it as a way to benefit the manufacturer, but we should say that the product becomes more efficient, and hence, the means to the product - that is, the production - become more efficient.

Haskell: Why?

Detmar: The manufacturer is the life entity, and the

production is the left side of the equation and the product on the right side is the Reward - or the interim Reward on its way to becoming the consumer product.

Haskell: OK.

Detmar: The efficiency allows the life or corporeal entity to either produce as much with less sacrifice or with the same sacrifice to produce more; and hence, for the producing individual person or corporation the employment of the efficiency of this opportunity of a better (that is, more productive) labor situation is a natural proclivity as we all want to survive and bring ourselves up away from misery.

Haskell: And so far it is an a-ethical situation. According to our previous discussion on ethics we know that when just one person is involved there are no ethical situations as that which is ethical requires at least two entities in order to create a social situation. Without a society, there is no ethic. Ethics requires at least two entities and an understanding as we averred in one of our previous interviews.

Detmar: Correct.

Haskell: But my question involves whether introducing an influx of labor to an existing community changing the balance of the wealth of the individuals - in this case driving the price of labor down - can be ethical. Can the purposeful introduction of plentiful labor, driving the value of the livelihood of many down causing them misery, be an ethical action? And actually, now that I think about it, the answer to this question could be applied to any of the components of the sacrifice expression thus indicating a solution to the age old quandary of whether mercantilism is ethical. That is, should the introduction of foreign goods be allowed into a society if they place pressure on the constituent producers to lower their profit margins or look to obtain cheaper labor thereby causing some misery, which is, of course, not good, because we know from our study of ethics that we must be cooperative and respectful of others for the purpose of producing in order to survive and take us away from misery?

Detmar: Yes.

Haskell: Then, how can a society be ethical if it is allowed to freely displace its labor through promoting immigration thereby upsetting the society's working people? In relating this question to the other factors of the sacrifice equation, how can we allow the introduction of informational technology allowing one person to be more informed and efficient (eventually) than another; how can we allow the influence of another society which has more information or works harder by applying more effort to its sacrifices than ours to enter our workplaces upsetting our society's constituents? It appears that I am wondering about the ethical justification with an economical outlook to allow for inequality. Even further and more importantly, what is the nature of the ethicality of the open market system as opposed to a society that emphasizes equanimity or what I suppose I could label "socialism" or even "communism"? I expect that the answer to this question of whether economic immigration can be an ethical thing or not will enable us to derive a solution to the subsequent inquiries.

Detmar: Again, phew! First, we need to review our understanding of ethics, then separate out the frames of relevancy for the individual issues of ethics that are entwined here in your interrogatives.

Haskell: In reviewing our previous interview when we discussed at length the nature of ethics, we know that ethics is the recognition of good in behavior and the good is based in survival; that which promotes our survival is the basis for that which is good. The element of that which promotes our survival for the purpose of cooperation which promotes production within behavior is respect. This respect enables us to cooperate socially, to live together, and allows us to produce things that promote our betterment: it is needed both socially and economically.

Detmar: I am glad you pointed out that respect has two functional aspects. Besides allowing us to cooperate to produce things that will allow for a better life that will take us away from misery which we can term economic respect, there is the social respect that allows us to be together for the purpose of fulfilling our behaviorally interactive requirements. We work to receive fulfillment of material things that make us physically comfortable, and also, we work to receive stimuli that give us cerebral solace, and this represents our social life. We make sacrifices both for physical and cerebral goodness and pleasure. Respect is the ingredient in our behavior that allows us to cooperate with each other to fulfill these two goals.

Haskell: Yes, I understand this, and it fits with the published discussion on ethics that we had, but I do not yet see how this will bring clarity to my question on the ethics of economics and more specifically on the introduction of inequality to a peaceful socio-economic situation.

Detmar: Our social and economic situations present us with two types of life entities each: first is the single entity, or the individual, and the second is the corporate entity, or the individuals en masse acting as one.

Haskell: I can see these situations: the economic individual producing his food by himself, the corporation, or cooperative, producing large quantities of food through the cooperation of many; and on the social side, the individual interacting with another to start a family, and the group banning together to form a club to play a sport which will interact with another club.

Detmar: The ethics that govern what is good for the single life entity is also good for the corporate body whether economic or social. If a body acts en masse, then it is a single entity, and our understandings that determine that ethics is based on respect of the other individuals with which it cooperates will be applicable to the corporeal mass entity as well.

Haskell: I can agree with this as this follows from our established and published understanding of ethics .

Detmar: And its obligations of respect which form the ethical are directed outward to other entities. Respect and ethical behavior principally involve the relationship between entities. As we pointed out in a previous conversation, ethics has limited relevancy to the lone individual. The first obligation of the individual is to survive and take itself away from misery. It tries to produce, and when it cannot live up to this expectation of itself, it will loose respect for itself. In order to produce cooperatively, respect is exported to other entities for the intention of cooperation which is for the purpose of material production to make us physically comfortable, and for social interaction respect is for cerebral pleasure.

Haskell: I'm listening.

Detmar: It is the export of respect from the consciousness that indicates that the consciousness will cooperate with the physical self to produce, and the giving of respect to other entities indicates that the entity is willing to cooperate with others for the purpose of production of material things or social interaction. It is this guideline of respecting all those with whom we have need or want to cooperate that we must adhere to when judging the ethics of an economic or social situation.

Haskell: I agree. And to summarize, the consciousness exports respect first to the self which we would term "self-respect" which allows us to cooperate with our physical self. Next, we have the respect which we export to other individuals that indicates our willingness to cooperate to produce physical things or social pleasure. On a secondary level when we group together en masse for either physical production or social pleasure, we have the respect that is exported to the other mass entities such as the companies that work together to sell and manufacture to each other ultimately producing consumer goods and services. And, I suppose, within these mass entities because, as you stated, they act as a single entity, there must also exist a self-respect analogous to the self-respect that the individual has for his physical and mental self.

Detmar: Yes, good point, Haskell. We also know that it is an absolute that we exist, and with this existence we have the will to survive and promote our existence and get us away from misery. Within these parameters we are sovereign; that is, each living entity owns its right to survive and promote its survival in this God given world. And in this context the consciousness of the entity will export respect to effect cooperation to promote its survival. We do not choose to come into existence with this will to survive; therefore, within this worldly predicament the ownership of our consciousness and the will to survive is totally ours: we are total sovereign owners of our conscious existence and our will to survive and prosper. We can only choose a cessation of our consciousness should risk and misery combine to induce us to such an unfortunate choice. Hence, any interdiction of this situation is against all of nature.

Haskell: I think I see.

Detmar: The life entity must make decisions in order to live: it must decide to eat, breath, think, act sociably, survive, and bring itself up away from misery. With its discovery that it is sentient comes the necessary requirement to make decisions. Hence, inherent to our very predicament we have ownership of our decision making abilities; otherwise, life could not begin to exist and sustain itself.

Haskell: Yes, I agree; it would be hard not to. But wait; outside of man the rest of the animal kingdom are DNA eaters and interdiction into the survival of another is a common course. Why should man's predicament be different as conflicts in the interest to survive arise?

Detmar: A conflict of interest is competition. But even in nature for any life entity there is the sovereign right to one's own existence and to promote it. Of course, it may run into the contrary interests of another and a life ending incident may ensue. But, I am indicating that the extinction of life, without cause of interest which in a social situation would necessitate the need for cooperation and therefore the invention and exportation from the self of respect, would be aberrant. It is within the group of life entities that requires the tool of cooperation to live and prosper that this right to survival extends outside itself into the group with its common interests which uses the vehicle of respect to promote and pursue its own happiness. It is to the group of common interest that has the will and need to cooperate and to which we can extrapolate the right to unencumbered existence.

Haskell: I think I see. Within the relevancy of the non-cooperative existence of a single entity, such as a lone shark in the sea, there is no common interest, and hence, his right to existence extends to the point where it comes into conflict with a competing interest. And when there is a group of entities with a common interest, the need for cooperation arises and the sovereign right to existence extends outside the entity to the group as it is in the interest of the group to recognize - that is, to be respectful of - the individuals as they have importance for the group. And so it is for this reason that it is wrong for private or political murder to occur and it cannot be justified.

Detmar: Yes. Because the individual is sovereign within the group to pursue the promotion of his survival, unless he gives up his right to choose for the betterment of his life, the group cannot override this sovereignty unless, of course, the society is in extreme jeopardy and there is a risk of its perishing or at least the amount of misery is overwhelmingly great. I think we covered this type of situation in detail in our interview on ethics and then on truth which you published.

Haskell: Yes. I remember the explanation clearly. It is the total dispensation of misery that decides the overall direction of decisions of the group and for the individual alike. But let's continue with the prosecution of this thought line to get us to a conclusion for my questions regarding the allowance of inequality into the group ecology situation.

Detmar: To continue, the individual has sovereignty over his own existence and its promotion; therefore, the individual may seek means to produce for himself and his family such as our enterprising inventor of the tool that we spoke of earlier in this discourse. Or he may justifiably send out signals of his willingness to cooperate with others to produce or trade production in concert.

Haskell: And why is he justified?

Detmar: He is justified in that he has absolute claim to the objective of the promotion of his survival. If he has not passed this sovereignty of choice on to another entity, then it remains with him, and hence, we have the justification of the sanctity of the existence of property rights.

Haskell: Hey, this is starting to sound like Locke and subsequently, Rousseau.

Detmar: Yes, it is because they had it right. As the individual has the sovereign right to choose for himself and to promote his survival, he has the inherent right to the results of his own choices which means he may own things unless he delegates this sovereignty of choice or part of it to another entity which would control the results of the choices instead. But if he has not delegated these choices and his right to elect, they remain with him. It would be unethical to forcibly take the choice and the results of these elections away from the individual.

Haskell: Therefore, the individual owns the means to his production such as his labor and his ingenuity, and he owns the results of this unless otherwise given up voluntarily in exchange for something else.

Detmar: Precisely, and hence, the derivation of the

ethicality of the free market system.

Haskell: But are not both the free market system and communism both ethical? One may just choose between the two.

Detmar: As the individual has sovereignty over his choices first, communism can only be ethical and right if the sovereign entity gives up voluntarily his right to make choices for his life and the results of his choices to be those of everybody within the society that is cooperating together. If they all cooperate to produce in concert and the results are decided to be equally proportioned, then communism is perfectly ethical due to the volitional evolution of a contract. It is ethical only after the sovereign choice is given up. If a new entity such as a child is born, grows up, and becomes a producer, the new worker cannot be placed into the communal sharing of production without his release of the right to choose. Therefore, the free market is first in its relevancy to the individual, and the sovereign individual may upon seeing that the promotion of his survival may be better effected if he allows the results to his choices and efforts to belong to the group as a whole with whom he is cooperating and for whom they are cooperating and extending their cooperative production also. The sovereignty rests with the individual first, then the group derives its rights from those given up by his free will.

Haskell: It would seem that Locke (or Rousseau) would agree with this: it is characteristic of his doctrine. But how does this relate to inequality in an economic system?

Detmar: It is the sovereignty of the individual: when there is an inequality due to opportunity (a derivative of risk), the employment of effort, or free will, the economic entity has the absolute right to choose for itself, promote its well being, and take itself away from misery. Due to its sovereignty it may choose to keep its wealth, and due to its innate, absolute propensity to live and take itself away from misery, it may utilize the advantage of its wealth whether accidentally or well directed and strived for without obligation to another.

Haskell: Yes, as we mentioned in the conversation on ethics, the world is run on sacrifice, risk, effort, and time, and, of course, we need to include the information/knowledge complex. But let's get back to being respectful to yourself and whether it relates to the corporate entity being respectful to itself such as in management being respectful to its employees. History shows us that sometimes they are not respectful, and therefore, not ethical to their employees. Let's take the situation of the company taking the cheaper labor situation that we discussed. How does one judge this predicament?

Detmar: We must take the standard of ethics that we have already propounded which is that ethics is behavior that is respectful for the purpose of cooperation to produce goods and services on the economic side and cerebral pleasure on the social side. The free will of the consciousness will weigh the success of our individual and its ability to produce, and if successful, the consciousness will laud the self (or in the case of the others in its society when noticing their success at production will laud that successful person) to an appropriate degree with respect.

Haskell: I see. And such should be the case of the corporate entity as with one's own self. We weigh our success at producing that which we strive for, and should we reach those goals, we are respectful of ourselves; and in a corporate situation the management would be respectful of the employees and adherence to the appropriate action would be that which is ethical. But, what if we are not able to produce or achieve our goals and something happens? Let's say, chance steps in and something prevents us. We are no worse as individuals. We failed not for trying but because of circumstances. Should we have no need of respect and therefore ethics?

Detmar: Of course not. However, as we discussed in more detail in our previous interlocution on ethics, we cannot respect them for their production; we have respect for them as individuals who strive for a purpose the best they can and this effort commands respect.

Haskell: Well, if we do not give as much respect to one person such as the unemployed person as the president of a company or country, can we say that we do not need as much ethical behavior toward one person as another?

Detmar: Ethics is the study of the disproportionate appropriation of respect to an individual. Cooperation is dependant on the dispensation of respect. As we should recall from our previous discussion and your published notes, ethics is the concern of the amount of respect that is dispensed in relation to the cooperation and whether it is appropriate or not.

Haskell: This review is instructive. Respect is behavior that the entity uses to effectuate cooperative behavior which we need in order to produce something. Ethics is the study or observation of this respect which enables us to cooperate, and if our conscience approves the amount of dispensation of the respect to the individual with whom we have the objective to cooperate, then we would term the action ethical. If the dispensation of respect is inappropriate and diminished below the amount of respect that the entity deserves, then the action which holds the diminished respect would be seen as unethical.

Detmar: Right. And the reason we need to accord others in our society our respect is that we have indicated an intention to cooperate and the understanding of the will to cooperate is known as a "right." Without the existence of an understanding of some sort of cooperation there can be no right, that is, there would be no right to respect.

Haskell: Yes, I recall our disquisition on ethics. So, let us get back to the problem of self-respect. How do we solve the problem of the company supplanting one worker for another due to the second one willing to work for less?

Detmar: The company must produce profitably or else it will not be able to survive and would not have any self-respect. It will replace or adjust whatever elements it needs to be able to succeed. Living entities strive to promote their interests and the conflict of such is competition.

Haskell: I'll accept that.

Detmar: Of course, because the human elements of the company are cooperating with each other within the organization, the company management must pay respect for this cooperation. They do so on two levels: first is that they pay a remunerative consideration usually in the form of money (but it can be in goods and services); secondly, when interacting with the employees they will pay them the respect due on a socially professional level. And, because the management recognizes the ongoing extent of cooperative behavior in the organization, they pay the respect and are ill-disposed to supplant this ongoing cooperative behavior without a due and considerable disruptive reason to which would indicate there is a problem that is posing a disruption of some magnitude to the interest of the company in producing its goods or services. We may call this the "economic or social cell," and like a living cell, it has a membrane, and in order to disrupt or change the cell you will need to pierce this outer protective wall of ongoing cooperation that is built of mutual respect.

Haskell: I see. Well, let's get to this problem of immigration and mercantilism. To reiterate, I am speaking, as an example, of two different societies separated by a boundary of some sort, and my question of immigration and inequality presupposes a discrepancy in the standard of living between the two, and if the lower one were to be allowed to migrate to the higher one, would the standard of living of the higher one fall or overall would it become more successful or prosperous? I know that for the single corporate entity its prosperity will increase due to the efficiency of the lower labor cost, but will the society on the whole benefit?

Detmar: Since we have described the economic decision in the form of a quantified expression, we can find the answer to this question.

Haskell: This will be interesting.

Detmar: If there are two equilibratory societies each trading back and forth, our equation, as it stands, can satisfy this situation. (If it is not in equilibrium, we will need the added features that calculus can bring to the equation in order to obtain quantifiable results.) Let us take a simple example of some participants. A group of farmers raises individually a particular type of crop such as wheat, carrots, cucumbers, tomatoes, and leaks. If from outside this xenophobic group, a farmer across the river and separated from the group makes a visit to his nearest neighbor after fording the river with his new product, potatoes. This farmer sends out information of the will to cooperate and of the benefits of potatoes. It is a difficult sale, but the farmer of the carrots who trades with the others for their products, in order to balance his diet, comes to realize that potatoes have significant nutritional benefits and would further the balance and quality of his family's diet. Thus, this carrot farmer comes to agree with the potato farmer that it is in his best interests to open up trade with him even though he is across the river, a cultural outsider. But he sees the benefits to himself and is convinced that potatoes will improve his life and promote his society.

Haskell: OK.

Detmar: But before he does, he communicates to the others in the group of his decision, and they, at least initially, object to this pending economically selfish action of the carrot farmer because they know that if the farmer of the carrots spends some of his production to buy or trade for potatoes, there will be less available to trade with them and they would like to get their usual quantities of carrots for their diets. But, in addition they are worried about the leek farmer because they know that the carrot farmer cares for leeks the least and they are concerned that the carrot farmer will use all his production for the potatoes, wheat, cucumbers, and tomatoes and leave little or none for the leeks fellow, and hence, he will not have enough carrots for his family to eat.

Haskell: This is an example of a classic protectionist situation. They are protecting one for a dubious benefit because if they all start eating potatoes it is obvious that their lives will be enhanced. Of course, even if the new entrant becomes a participant, the others would probably increase their production, if they could, to absorb the new entrant thereby contributing to the group growth. But let us suppose the situation is as it is. How can we prove that such behavior is not good to pursue as a policy?

Detmar: We can know because each economic cell has an ongoing degree of cooperation inherent within it (as expressed as a coefficient of effort in the equational expression), and when it is disrupted and realigns itself, it does so because of the introduction of an efficiency.

Haskell: Really? How's that?

Detmar: The potential for growth is the impetus for change of the economic condition, and growth is driven in two ways: by efficiency and quantity of the economic cells otherwise known as our economic decision as described by the equational expression.

Haskell: In our present case of the produce farmers we have both ingredients.

Detmar: But even though just increasing the number of participants contributes to the overall quantity of the group, it does nothing for the rate per capita for effort which truly indicates whether we are proceeding away from misery. Only efficiency can do this and it is described as Risk X Time X Information X Effort times its coefficient of capital equaling the Sacrifice or in its final form, the Consumer Reward.

Haskell: What? Capital is a kind of efficiency? You mentioned a bit ago that a capital good is a mechanical effort created from our rationalities and knowledge.

Detmar: Yes. And the result of that mechanical effort is an efficiency in the form of effort and a mass. Any capital good or service is nothing but an efficiency to produce a desideratum. If we desire something new - it could be anything - the means to it is through a change in capital and this amounts to a form of efficiency. The making of a tool such as a hunting apparatus is the product of the free will operating on the information factor by adding the technology of the bow and arrow to the hunter that enables him to become more efficient in the obtainment of food.

Haskell: Surely there are capital goods or services that are not examples of efficiencies such as a television.

Detmar: Even a television is an efficient means to bring entertainment to the self at home. Its invention increased the efficiency of the entertainment industry. The capital item is an extension of effort, and any addition or invention of a new piece of capital has the purpose of increasing the efficiency of production. Capital is the mechanical extension of effort, and a differentiation of capital is the increase of its efficiency.

Haskell: What about land? It is capital, but land does not demonstrate by itself any efficiency.

Detmar: Land is the mechanical means to produce the farmer's commodities to eat and buildings to live in, and the effort to obtain its ownership is a key foundation to wealth. Its efficiency lies in the fact that it is key to producing food and the space to build dwellings to live on. Its greatest efficiency was when agriculture was discovered through our creativity producing knowledge and brought man out of the hunting and gathering stage, but, granted, it does not differentiate well, and hence, an increase in efficiency comes hard fought but occasionally happens when people sometimes moderate difficult land such as mountainsides by terracing, irrigation, or fertilizing, all examples of differentiating land to make it more efficient as a means to produce. More recently, the knowledge of biotechnology is adding further efficiencies

Haskell: I see.

Detmar: And the use of the land derives itself from our priority to produce food and get someplace to live. We make an effort to produce food and find someplace to live and one of the mechanical means of our effort manifests itself as land. Land is the extension of our effort, and we use it as a tool because it increases our efficiency in producing food and providing someplace to live. In every case we can trace the appearance of capital back to an efficiency in effort to the purpose of a sacrifice.

Haskell: I think I understand. So in the case of that potato farmer, we see in the product the efficiency in the delivery of two things: first, we understand the increase of nutritional benefits and the added pleasure of the taste.

Detmar: And we may add this potato capital to the equation and it will deliver the quantification of the Reward. It will note that the Risk X the Information X the Time (to produce the crop) X the Effort (along with any capital and cooperative coefficients) equals a competitive score on the product comparative to other produce, and hence, the potential for a market niche develops, and as such, along comes the potato farmer from away to try to develop it, that is, to fulfill a human need that will improve life and take us farther away from misery.

Haskell: And how would we integrate the unequal efficiency into this equation?

Detmar: Efficiency is the positive differentiation of any of the equative factors (usually this is generated by the creative abilities of the free will of the capital); hence, to use the concepts of calculus, the difference between the capital at one point in time minus the capital at a second point in time divided by the difference in time would measure the increase of an efficiency, and we might note this as dc/dt. And if we include the positive differentiations of all the equational factors, we could say df/dt.

Haskell: OK. And how can we determine whether it

is beneficial for the society as a whole?

Detmar: If we add up the individual transactions of the potato farmer selling his product to each of the participants, there will develop a quantification by its sum that will compare favorably to the adding up of the transactions without the potatoes.

Haskell: OK. If we add up the potato transactions, we will get a total indicating overall satisfaction, and the sum of the satisfaction of the Rewards will be greater than the sum of the previous set without him.

Detmar: Yes, but the critical point is that it must add up to the degree that the differential of an added benefit will be greater than the corresponding decrease in the loss of the business to the leek farmer thus providing an overall increase.

Haskell: So we could say that there is a net benefit to society if we allow the inequality of the advantages that the potato farmer possesses to join the society of farmers across the river.

Detmar: Yes. We could describe this as the sum of the potato transactions less the sum of the original set of transactions is greater than the sum of the original transactions less these original transactions without the leek farmer transactions indicating an overall increase to the benefit of society as a whole.

Haskell: And hence, if we look at the problem from an ethical point of view, we see that although one individual, due to the risk of his situation, is in jeopardy of losing some short term production, the overall good to society is improved, and hence, an ethical action for man because it demonstrates an increase of respect overall and brings society further away from misery.

Detmar: Yes. If the total benefit to the four farmers is great enough to overcome the deficit that will be experienced by the one, then it is an obvious overall benefit. Of course, if we add in the benefit that the potato farmer will receive, then it furthers the overall societal benefit especially if we count him as part of the group.

Haskell: Can we relate this method of calculation to the justification of the appearance and toleration of inequality?

Detmar: Naturally. With the appearance of inequality, one becomes better than another, and the good of the higher inequality, when we enter the economic situation, will always benefit to the group over time (given the absence of political intervention). The proof of this is in the above process. If an disproportionate good appears, over time it will produce something good, and when it does, this good will, because of the self-interest inherent in promoting one's own survival by trading with others, proceed to operationally pervade society and add on overall good.

Haskell: Wow! Do you realize also that you have just equated inequality with the good and with efficiency? I believe Herbert Spencer initiated an idea along this line of thought.

Detmar: The appearance of an inequality is representative of an added efficiency in the economic situation, and in the social state the inequality is representation of the degree of respect in the analogous situation.

Haskell: How so?

Detmar: The good in the economic situation is determined by that which promotes goods and services which takes us away from misery and adds to the quality of life. The appearance of an unequal situation dictates that something is better in the economic sense than another and that which has the greater good has a greater efficiency in producing a good or service.

Haskell: Naturally.

Detmar: And socially, what is good is that which is cooperative, and production depends on cooperation which requires respect as we have discussed.

Haskell: That fits. But what about the example where the farmers are dealing in products that are not equal in value and the situation becomes complicated and bartering becomes awkward and time consuming? We will want to calculate the quantitative expression: we will need the vehicle of money. And what about the classic mercantilistic situation of exporting to get the other country's money or gold?

Detmar: Money is just a quantity of promissory notes that represent that which society has produced. Money is conditional upon production: without production money cannot exist. And to add this to our equation, all we need to do is multiply both sides of the equation by whatever denomination we might choose. Hence, in the British mercantilism times the politicos thought if Britain could export more than they imported (and this thought remains to some degree currently still in many areas), they would be net receivers of wealth. However, it is no matter whether they received the compensation for the exports in gold, silver, pounds, francs, or whatever: money by whatever name represents past, present, or future production, and if Britain exported goods to France and received gold or some other form of money, it is because France produced or would produce something. If she did not, the French would have no gold, their francs would have little or no worth.

Haskell: Yes, you are right. Even in the not too distant past, politicos and a few economic mavens fretted over whether the trade deficit with the Far East was hurting the U.S. economically.

Detmar: That's right. But foreign countries will send their goods only if we produce something substantive that somebody can buy with the U.S. currency that goes out of the country. If this currency goes out, it can only be valued if there is somebody out there that will buy the U.S. dollar back (at a discount, of course) and is confident that this will bring goods and services produced by someone in the U.S. If there is no one producing anything, then that holder of the dollar cannot buy anything and it becomes valueless.

Haskell: Hence, exchange rates would be a powerful gauge of production and the value of a country's currency.

Detmar: Yes.

Haskell: And mercantilism as an abstract objective is without reason.

Detmar: Of course.

Haskell: Well, let's get back to our little mercantilistic farmers' economy. I understand the concept of money and its incorporation into our equational expression, but what about fluctuations of its value as noted in the price of things? How can we note price and its fluctuations into our modular expression?

Detmar: The determination of the value of the Sacrifice, or the Reward, is initially determined by the product side of the equation and finally and precisely by the sacrifice side of the equation, or by the buyer, and hence, the equation will develop as follows: Money x (RTEI) proceeds to, as we substitute RTEI for the Reward, Money X (Reward) X Priority(Supply Side) = Price(Initial).

Haskell: What on earth are you talking about? What happened to the law of supply and demand which is what I thought determined the price? What happened with that? Is the law of supply and demand not true; does it not explain one of the most basic truisms of economic theory?

Detmar: Economists have used it because it seems to fit many situations in economic problems, but it is not a law because it is not always true; and an economy does not always operate according to this explanation, and therefore, it is not an economically universal law. The law of supply and demand is an invalid statement although it has been very helpful as it is applicable in understanding many economic problems.

Haskell: This is one your most surprising statements.

Detmar: Not at all. There are many instances where this law cannot explain the behavior of the economy because it ignores the mechanics of behavior. Another recent example of the inconsistency of the law is in the computer industry where demand is growing as exhibited by the industry's tremendous sales increases yet prices are dropping. Economic texts cite other rules that they layer on top of the law of supply and demand such as the theory of elasticity of demand which produces variations of price.

Haskell: This example of the computer industry has extenuating circumstances because the growth of supply is probably outstripping the growth in demand. Also, involved with this marketplace is the explosion of technology.

Detmar: Demand is up, sales are increasing, and the market for information equipment is exploding; costs are dropping. This law of supply and demand cannot explain it, entirely and completely, therefore it is not a law at least not in the sense that Plank's Constant is invariable or the Second Law of Thermodynamics is a law.

Haskell: Well, please explain. I do not even know what to ask you first to explain about this subject.

Detmar: Price determination ultimately is a twofold process. First, the manufacturing process, that is, the first part of the equation, determines the initial proposed cost, and this cost is inherent in the information factor. The producer has determined through the operation of his free will upon the available information of the completion of the proposed sacrifice and reward that his productions will fill a probable need (I say "probable" due to the existence of risk in all situations), and its completion is estimated at a certain level of effort, and this effort has a certain value or worth that the producer has placed nominally on the proposed sacrifice-reward.

Haskell: I think I understand this placement of a value upon the sacrifice, but is it just composed of effort? Capital is not included?

Detmar: Remember, all capital is a derivative of effort; it is an extension of the efficiency placement of effort. All capital is used to make our efforts easier and our pleasure greater.

Haskell: Yes, I remember.

Detmar: Hence, price is initially determined on a cost analysis of the product.

Haskell: But the price situation must be different for a product that is coming on the market with several other competing products than will one that is unique and has no competition; and in addition, there must be an impact on the price if the buyer has much incentive to purchase the product and the demand for the product is increasing.

Detmar: If there are others purveying the same product, then this information, when realized, will be part of the initial price calculations. The overriding essential consideration is that his production will be received with considerations that will be commensurate with his exertions. He must to his satisfaction know that in order to proceed with his efforts and the extensions of its various types of capital to secure an objective sacrifice, his production will ultimately be consumed by either himself or others, and if others, then he should secure consideration that will be worthy of his efforts.

Haskell: Then, it is not an issue if there is competitive company. The only consideration is that a price can be set according to the amount of his effort and the buyer's priorities. If the market level does not provide enough consideration for the market researcher, he will either decline entrance or just produce for private consumption such as is the case for a private garden. The important point, it seems, is that the decision to produce its price will be on the left side of the equation which indicates the producer's decisions.

Detmar: Correct. On the product reward side of the equation the decision to acquire arises which will indicate the acceptance of the product as fulfilling a need that promotes our survival and takes us away from misery. However, the fulfillment of the need by the cooperative payment of a consideration for the product which ultimately must come from either a past, present, or future production of an ultimately consumable product must fit the buyer's priorities (even if the producer and buyer are one and the same person and we are producing something for one immediate person's consumption). That is, if the price set by the manufacturer is thought to be high, it is because the buyer feels that the consideration needed to acquire the product is too dear which is dictated by his previously established priorities which is a form of knowledge as discussed in our previous conversation on truth. As we have a limited amount of assets which are established by how much we have produced, am producing, or will manufacture, we must prioritize how we will utilize these assets and this is expressed by introducing the factor of priorities to the Reward side of the equation. Hence, we have: M(RTE(C)I) X Priority = (Rwd)M X Priority = Price.

Haskell: So the price is secondarily dictated by the reception of the product set against a factor of priorities which dictate the value of the product to the buyer.

Detmar: Yes.

Haskell: We need to go over this concept comprehensively as it is vague in my mind, and it seems to somewhat clash with the time honored rule of supply and demand.

Detmar: Not really. Supply is the left side of the equational expression which equals the production. The demand side of the equation will be the Reward (or product) times its Priorities which also equals the price when multiplied by the money coefficient. When the mutual priorities allow the cooperative considerations (the price) of both sides to meet and exchange, a transaction occurs; that is, a deal is struck.

Haskell: But information should be on the right side of the equation, the demand side. As it reads only "reward times priority," it would seem that information is not present as it is on the other side, and I feel that a consumer in making his decision to buy the product, that is, to allocate his pent up assets of the past, present, or future production to obtain the reward must have taken in information in order to decide.

Detmar: He did. A priority itself is the result of a mental decision which is Information (and previously established knowledge together) times Risk times Mental Effort multiplied by Time. This produces a mental decision that brings forth a priority which is a piece of knowledge which is based on that which is good for us, the good being a value that promotes our survival.

Haskell: I am confused. I do not have everything straight in my mind.

Detmar: OK. Let's review. First, we should recall some things from our previous discussion, the notes of which you put to print and entitled it <u>Truth & The Nature of Decisions</u>. We know from that disquisition that:

- Information is stimuli plus memory,

- Knowledge is the free will plus information (or previous knowledge) within a relevant reference,

- Free will is reason + will,

- Priorities are free will + information + mental action,

- A value = knowledge of that which is good (a good is that which promotes survival and takes us away from misery), and

- A decision is that which is in the arena of the consciousness which assigns a priority through the means of the free will based on preferences of the good which is based in survival in order to probably effect an action which has a desired return which is a sacrifice.

In this interview we have reduced the calculation of a decision to Risk X Effort X Information/Knowledge X Time, the individual factors being assigned their quantities by the free will.

Haskell: But I thought this was the Sacrifice.

Detmar: It is. But we have various degrees of the Sacrifice. The most basic is the mental Sacrifice which is the mental decision to do something or to know something. Hence, a mental decision is Risk (we include risk even though at this level it is slight but still existent) X Time X (Information + Knowledge of previously established priorities) X Mental Effort = A New Priority (a Sacrifice). At the next level of complication we would include physical effort as well. This would be described by the expression: Risk X Time X Knowledge/Information X Mental and Physical Efforts = The Reward (which is a physical manifestation of a sacrifice). If the reward requires various and many steps to produce, such as an automobile, we need to include capital and land into the ingredients of the equation as noted anon. We also know that these terms within the equational expression can be delineated by dimensional units just as other equations in physics and chemistry are.

Haskell: Yes. I understand this. If we include them in the expression of the production of a product we get: Risk X Time(sec) X Knowledge/Information(bytes) X Mental/Physical Effort(man units) = the Reward(bytes-man-sec). And if we include the coefficient of capital which we can differentiate out of Effort, we get:

R X T(hours) X Knowledge(bytes) X Effort(ergs or man units) X Capital(efficiency mass units) = Reward(efficiency mass units-erg-byte-hours) which is conceptually possible.

Detmar: Correct. And to proceed further we know that within the mechanics of the decision making process we have the previously established priorities in memory that are of our knowledge that we actively use to prosecute our decisions into final actions. If we differentiate out the priorities from the equational expression and separate them from the rest of the knowledge that we use in the decision making process, we can express it as:

C X I X R X E X T X Priority (of the supply

side) = the Reward X Priority (demand)

We further remember that the single priority is a mental decision producing knowledge of what is good for us which we noted as

R x I/K(bytes) X T(hours) X E(mental effort or mental erg units) = New Knowledge = The Mental Sacrifice = The Priority

Haskell: OK

Detmar: If we divide both sides of the equation by our previously established priorities, that is, we divide the supply side by the demand priority and the reward side by the supply priority, and if we divide both sides by risk and time (because if we perform a transaction it will become a fait accompli and risk and time are no longer present after a purchase), we get

C(efficiency mass unit) X I/K(bytes) X R X T(hours) X E(physical effort units) X E(mental effort units) / T(hours) X R X E(mental effort) X I/K(bytes)

= Reward(efficiency mass unit-bytes-hrs-physical-mental effort) / Priority(supply)

= C(efficiency mass unit) x E(physical units)

= Reward

and if we multiply both sides by the money factor, we get the price of the reward/product which is the subject of the transaction.

Haskell: What! Let's go through this conceptually because although I see what you did with the equations, I cannot follow how it relates to the real world.

Detmar: We have spoken of the law of supply and demand and the elasticity of demand, and economic texts have indicated that both theories are needed to determine price.

Haskell: Yes.

Detmar: We know that supply and demand cannot determine the fluctuations in price without fail, but it usually follows that when there is an increase in supply without a corresponding increase in demand, the price will fall; and conversely when the supply drops the price will surely rise; and on the other side of the coin when demand rises without the corresponding rise in supply, the price will rise usually, and when the demand diminishes, the cost will usually go down.

Haskell: Yes, it does not follow perfectly as demand has elasticity so that if the price goes up the consumer may switch to other products. And if the price goes down, it may or may not attract further purchases.

Detmar: This elasticity of demand is due to the existence of the priority in our decision making process. The priority is the value of that which is good for us and a series of priorities establishes the relative value which sets the price of the object of the transaction in conjunction with the amount of supply.

Haskell: I am still not sure I understand.

Detmar: We can say that the price of a product is set by the relative positions of the supply and demand relative to the priorities of the supplier and demander. If the priority of a product is conducive to a high value of importance such as food, which we obviously need to live, the price of food can rise due to a limited supply, and hence, demand may fall somewhat and seek alternate products, if possible. The demand for basic foods, no matter how high the price, will continue until supply meets demand due to the high prioritization of food. It is obvious people always need food. The limiting factor is whether people have enough money to purchase the food at all. This situation would have occurred during history's famines.

Haskell: Can we state the relationship between supply, demand, and priorities more precisely and possibly in an equational expression?

Detmar: Yes. We know that:

Priority(Supply) X (R)(T)(I)(E(C)) = Reward X Priority(Demand)

We just need to point out that there are two priorities - one of the supply side and one on the demand side. Their nature is the same; they are derived in the identical manner but from the different perspectives of the two sides of the equation. And hence, the final equational expressions to equalize the price of the transaction are:

M X (R)(T)(I)(E(Capital)) / Priority of Demand = Reward X M / Priority of Supply

which can be shortened to

M(RTE(C)I) / Priority(Demand) = (Reward)M / Priority(Supply) = Price

or

M(RTE(C)I) / RTEI(Demand) = (Reward)M / RTEI(Supply) = Price

We leave it to the mutual communications of the demander and the supplier to adjust and equalize the priorities so that the two sides of the equation will balance, establish a price, and effect a transaction.

Haskell: I see. But now I would like to ask a most important question which I have been thinking about since the topic of mercantilism popped up, but now it seems is the appropriate time.

Detmar: I am sure this will be both interesting and probably difficult to answer.

Haskell: I would like to know if what we have discussed has any final significance. Can it be useful? Can this subject matter be used to tell what is the best type of economy. Is a free and open economy better than a closed one? Is a partially closed economy such as what we see in the Far East better than a totally open one? Is it beneficial to put up tariffs on imports to help protect a domestic economy and is this more efficient to growth than a totally open economy? Is there a degree to which we should protect our domestic economy that should be implemented? Can what we have discussed be used to formulate policy and to know what is good for us and best for our overall societal survival? Even though we seemed to touch upon this subject when we spoke of mercantilism, I do not, as of yet, have any understanding of what is good for us economically. And in order for our discussion to have significance, we must be able to answer these questions.

Detmar: To be sure.

Haskell: I have some understanding of our interview, and I believe that in order to seek a solution to the interrogatives, we must start with the knowledge of the nature of economic growth as that economy which can grow most rapidly will be that which will benefit its subjects and facilitate their survival and take them up and away from misery.

Detmar: Yes, certainly.

Haskell: I know growth to be the differential of the output of our equational expression over time. In fact we could probably express this using calculus to further advance our expression.

Detmar: Yes, we sure could.

Haskell: And I know from basic economic texts that growth is often fueled by investment which is possible if there is profit.

Detmar: Yes. It starts with the nature of profit and what can generate it in the most facile manner.

Haskell: Perhaps if we start here at the nature of profit, we can come to an understanding and solution to my interrogatives.

Detmar: Yes. Profit is equational to the reward, or that is, the consumable reward as only the final objective, or the saved production to be realized later as a consumable, can be profit. We strive for profit to be able to purchase consumables now or in the future in order to further our survival and take us up and away from misery. All effort has an objective, and the aim can be either interim or final on its way toward its goal of achieving a reward. Everybody's ultimate aim is to obtain something that is of the good, id est, something that promotes their survival and brings them up and away from misery for themselves and those that will survive them.

Haskell: Yes. I agree. We strive and make sacrifices of all things we have discussed such as the sacrifice of our time and effort in order to receive some sort of reward that will promote our survival.

Detmar: Any time we are able to receive something that is pleasurable to our consciousness, promotes our survival, and banishes misery, we may call it profit. It is the profit of our sacrifice. And a company's profit is the same. It is for consumable usages either as a reward for its owners or for its own use which would take a portion of the profit of the company to spend on itself and its own well-being which we could call investment.

Haskell: Yes. That fits. And the investment part of the profit would be used to increase one of the constituents of our equation to increase its output and again enhance the profit picture of the right side of the equation and further satisfy the existent demand to its products.

Detmar: Yes.

Haskell: So how can we know which economic course to pursue in order to maximize the promotion of our survival and take us away from misery? Is there something to which we could refer to establish and understand a most efficient economic policy?

Detmar: Yes. If we examine how we make decisions and follow where our equational expression leads us, we will come to a conclusive policy, outlook, and standard by which we can answer your interrogatives.

Haskell: Really! This will be exciting.

Detmar: We know that all of life runs on risk, sacrifice, effort, information and knowledge, and free will over time, that all our decisions are produced within the consciousness which has the objective to effect an action with a desired return which is a sacrifice which will hopefully be good for us which is to promote our survival and take us away from misery.

Haskell: Yes, I understand.

Detmar: We further know that the decision making process is modular. This is described by our equational expression the basis of which is that Risk X Time X Information X Effort = A Sacrifice. And the economic expression of this would be to note that all capital is a derivative of effort and that all capital is an expression of efficiency in and of itself. Capital is generated by our effort for the lone purpose of enhancing the efficient production of goods and services in order to promote our survival and take us away from misery. Hence, within our expression capital is a derivative, and we note it as a coefficient of effort, and the ultimate purpose of the economic event is to produce a reward whether it be a good or service.

Haskell: I understand.

Detmar: And the word "profit" is nothing but that which is the reward of the sacrifice that we make to the purpose of our good. Should we want to increase our rewards to further promote our survival taking ourselves away from misery, that is, to do that which is good for us, we can only do it by either modulating the individual factors of growth or increasing the number of decisions that produce the quantity of sacrifices and rewards.

Haskell: Yes. We can increase or decrease the individual factors of the decision making process such as decreasing risk or time, or increasing effort or information and knowledge or by increasing the number of decisions either per capita or per the economy as a whole.

Detmar: But the most important growth is that which promotes our survival producing a higher standard of living on a per capita basis, and the means by which we can modulate the factors of the decision making process is to invest the profit back into the factors which by and large over time have produced advances in civilization and increased our standard of living.

Haskell: Yes, although it seems that these increases seem to come in spurts if we look at those periods of history that resulted in the standard of living increases, such as with the inception of agriculture, the invention of the printing press, or the advent of the industrial revolution; and perhaps now, we may be in another which we might call the revolution of the micro-chip as noted in the excellent tome by Michael Rothschild, *Bionomics*. But in any case, I understand your point in that we need to increase our efficiency to produce the reward and the quantity and variety.

Detmar: And the only sources of any increase in the individual components of the equational expression comes from either the free will or the surrounding environment. It is the free will which is made up of reason and mental effort that administers to the extent, that we can, the increase or decrease of these components voluntarily and the environment that brings the involuntary information, time, and risk.

Haskell: I understand why you qualify the statement

by saying "to the extent" because of the existence of risk that many times is beyond our influence to control although we can and do moderate much of it in our decisions.

Detmar: It is the reason and creative abilities that we possess that set up the equations and run them to produce these decisions that we need to make constantly to keep us alive and keep our consciousness going.

Haskell: So how does this conclusion help with my set of questions?

Detmar: It is key because when we have a problem, we need the free will with its reason and sentient effort to set up the equations to calculate and make the necessary decisions, and hence, the more free will available per problem, the better off in general the overall solutions will be. The greater the quality and integrity of the individual factors of the calculative equations due to the presence of reason and cerebral effort, the overall efficaciousness of the solutions and rewards.

Haskell: Hmmm.

Detmar: There are two parameters of the free will

entity: the intensity and excellence of the single free will and the number of free wills available. Sometimes numbers can make up for a lack of excellence in a single free will and sometimes a single excellent free will entity will further, or outperform, the success of many. But whatever the combination is in any problem, the greater the excellence of the free will, the greater the probability of it producing excellent equations that will influence our decisions. Therefore, with any problem we want the maximization of the free will to help insure the best possible solutions.

Haskell: I see.

Detmar: And so, when considering the problem of what economic system is inherently the best, the answer is that system that allows the greatest intensity and amount of free will to be applied to each of the economic problems that arise in the daily life of the economic person or entity.

Chapter 5 - The Dictum of Cooperative Relevancy

Haskell: I am still not quite clear as to where this is going.

Detmar: As the faculties of our reasoning and creative abilities attend to the incoming information and that knowledge which is available in memory to set up the equational calculations that will produce the conclusions that we need in order to initiate our actions, the accrual of free will - in order to be optimally efficacious - which is the progenitor of the sacrifices that promote our survival and keep us away from misery should be uninhibited.

Haskell: OK.

Detmar: In the case of an economic system, such as the free market, socialism, or communism, should one system allow more free will to attend to the number of the individual sacrifices, rewards, or transactions, that is, to allow a greater amount of free will per economic transaction, then the greater will be its efficiency as a whole, as an operational entity.

Haskell: Well then, is one system able to accrue more free will than another? It seems that if the number of people in two systems are about the same, then the average amount of available free will would be about the same.

Detmar: Yes, of course. But its use, direction, and application to the individual transactions may not be the same per transaction. In the free market each transaction has the adherence and attention of those persons or entities that are relevantly associated through self-interest which is that concern which is good for oneself and will promote its own survival and protect itself from the ubiquitous presence of the possibility of misery. If a decision can improve our existence, we have a relevant interest. And some decisions may require or invite all other free will entities that have a relevant interest in the forthcoming decision.

Haskell: Yes, many times a decision affects more than one person, and a group of people will be summoned to collectively consider the problem which would be the case frequently in business situations. Those people who are assigned a project will work together as a unit to complete the task.

Detmar: In a centrally planned or partially planned economy decisions for many are made by fewer people, and hence, the amount of free will per transaction lessens, and therefore, the efficaciousness of the overall number of transactions will decrease as the amount of risk increases overall.

Haskell: I see. As the amount of reason used in the overall economy decreases in a centrally planned economy, the effectiveness of the decisions required to effectuate the economy will naturally decrease. Or maybe I should say probably it will decrease unless of course there is a giant mind that is able to provide and support the decisions by its huge intensity that would allow the sum of its reasoning to outweigh the sum of the individual lesser minds with its smaller quantities and intensities of reason.

Detmar: Correct. And the same problem can happen not only to political entities which start to engulf the decisions normally made in the individual and private sector of an economy, but to large corporations when the upper management micro-manages the information and ongoings of the lesser echelons of the corporation. Should upper management overstep the bounds of the abilities of their free will by having the president whose history is in finance make personnel or design decisions, this would be a blatant example of insufficient, incompetent, free will applied to inappropriate, specific problems. But generally (I say "generally" because of the possibility of disaster that can be generated by the existence of risk in our universe), when a corporation's sales starts to sag, it is because of the mistreatment of the free will toward the incoming information or the ignoring of the incoming information whether it comes from without or up from the lower echelons of the company to the upper management. If the corporation has not set up properly the flow of information and the maximum application of the corporation's talent of free will, it will eventually begin to deteriorate in the face of competition.

Haskell: I see. Well, perhaps relevant to this policy of maximizing the free will in an economy, there can be applied the most important question of all for me though I recognize that we have already discussed this in a different vein to a satisfactory conclusion. This is whether this free will policy can be used to conclusively demonstrate that mercantilism in any form, or any restraint of trade whatever, especially the type used in the Far East in the past (and still currently) that promotes the internal production of consumer goods by the erecting of barriers to the consumer goods that could come from abroad is a viable economic growth policy. But as a class of problems I wonder whether any favorable prejudicial treatment by a political entity toward any internal industry that it wants to promote can be discovered to be a positive or a negative in its overall effects and conclusions?

Detmar: Good question. As we have already mentioned, there is the obvious point that the group that experiences the imposition of restricted trade no matter how ever slight will incur a decrease, or perhaps it is better said, will not be able to advance its standard of living as easily or smoothly as it would if it had no restrictions.

Haskell: Yes, we discussed that. If consumers have not been given the choices that they would otherwise select and they are not allowed access to certain products, then they would not be able to enjoy as high a standard of living as they could.

Detmar: If they are producing something, then they can purchase or engage in transactions, and if they would like to partake in a certain transaction but cannot because of the choice imposed upon them by another entity, typically a political entity, then they are not enjoying a standard of living that they otherwise could.

Haskell: Yes. It is just as our group of farmers would experience in our example of the inclusion of the farmer of potatoes from across the river.

Detmar: Secondly, if the present production which is attended to by the free will of the society is yoked to the present standard of living and production level, then this aggregate free will will not be allowed to pursue the new replacement products that the society would like to substitute instead of the ones that are actually desired due to their high quality or inexpensiveness or whatever. This condition will prevent the free will from pursuing the course that it would otherwise seek. The free will would not differentiate which is to apply its creative powers to other more involved and higher problems. It restrains the free will or yokes it to the present lower, less complicated products that it must necessarily produce to fill the gap instead of going past those to other problems and decisions that it will probably have to pursue anyway eventually.

Haskell: I see. The capture of the free will to keep it occupied to produce that which it would only be inferior, or at best mediocre, at least for a while, will prevent the society from being as great as its potential will allow it.

Detmar: Precisely. If its members are producing, then the members can buy consumables, and if the societal productive members are not allowed to place their money where they would like to, then their free will is not being allowed to some extent to be employed as it otherwise might, and hence, the aggregate free will cannot live up to its potential. The free will differentiates to lesser problems than it would otherwise be employed.

Haskell: And by differentiating you mean life's ability to be creative as we spoke about in our first discussion, as I reproduced and transcribed, in *The Nature of Aesthetics.*

Detmar: Yes. And any society that employs restriction of trade will in the long run remain behind the advancement and the standard of living of one that does not, all other circumstances and conditions being equal.

Haskell: What about political issues such as whether a society should allow welfare or a restriction on the trade of drugs. Is this restriction of the free will detrimental or helpful to society? I understand why many are hesitant about opening the market to illicit drugs, but I know there are a few liberal (and I use this word in the classical economic sense) economists that believe it is best to have no restrictions, that restrictions make the overall problem worse.

Detmar: The purpose of government is to help protect people from people. Some people do bad, and worse yet, sometimes even evil things, and if the members of society feel that in this instance people need to be protected from other people such as from a drug pusher, then it is a burden that the society will have to endure. But it does not obviate our rule: if there is a restriction, then there is a suppression of the free will; but in some cases society may vote to impose a sanction if it believes that due to the imperfections of man (a class or type of risk) sometimes man in the aggregate, must solicit his representative, the government, to impose a burden on the free will for the general protection of the society's members.

Haskell: I have another question which I feel is of considerable importance in obtaining an integrated understanding of your purports concerning the role of free will in decision making and in particular economic behavior: I am wondering whether this understanding can elucidate whether private enterprises can be known to be inherently more efficient then publicly or governmentally owned, or affiliated corporations and enterprises?

Detmar: Yes. Interesting. I perceive here that you are referring to a government owned corporation as a publicly owned corporation. I make note of this because of the much used term "publicly traded" which would refer to large private corporations whose equities trade freely on the exchanges.

Haskell: Yes. And I think that in theory that the nationally (or governmentally) owned, the private, and publicly traded corporation should be the same since they have the same organization, that is, the nationally owned corporation also would have a president, a board of directors, and stockholders. It is just that the stock is held by the public in the form of government representatives who would sit on the board of directors.

Detmar: Yes.

Haskell: And it would further seem that the private and governmentally owned corporations would have their interests guarded and adhered to equally well as their structures are the same, and there is no reason to suppose that the governmentally owned corporation's management would be any less sincere and devoted to upholding the success of the corporation than the privately owned company.

Detmar: Yes. I agree.

Haskell: It further seems that because the management of the government enterprise would have the same concerns as any other manager and would be devoted to the survival, promotion, and overall fiscal health of the governmental corporation as much as any other company, the governmental corporation should be able to compete with the private enterprise. In fact, it would seem that because of the ability of the public, or that is, the governmentally owned company to borrow at will and at the best rates because of the full faith of the government behind it, the governmentally owned corporation would have a slight upper hand in its pursuit of profit and success.

Detmar: It would seem so.

Haskell: But I have read in texts that government owned companies do not fare well compared to private enterprise and that it has been empirically shown that this is so: the private sector seems to always out perform the public sector.

Detmar: Yes. It does.

Haskell: I have seen some depictions of the problem that explain that it is because of the principle that it is easier to spend someone else's money than one's own, and because of this, management in the public enterprise sector would feel more at ease in spending money as their own survival and promotion of their life style is not at stake and would not be as fiscally responsible as those in the private sector. But I feel that this does not explain why the governmentally owned corporations do not have the creativity of the privately owned corporations. That is, they do not move as nimbly in response to market forces and competition and often have to be protected by tariffs and given special consideration by the government through protective measures, and even then, they often end up operating at a loss. So, I feel that there must be something further that we will need to add in order to effect explanation of this phenomenon.

Detmar: The answer lies in the information flows.

Haskell: Why would information flow differently between the public and private sector? They are both made up of human beings and if they pay their management equally well, the quality per capita of management will be on the average approximately the same. Secondly, how and why would the information and knowledge of the two types of companies flow differently? Is there any special underlying mechanism that causes this?

Detmar: The underlying cause is the mismanagement of the interplay between the free will and the information and knowledge which our priorities are of prime importance. In the case of the public sector and in the governmentally owned corporations throughout the world, the proper flow of the information, knowledge, and the priorities of the public company are interdicted by politics.

Haskell: What is this "proper flow" of information to which you refer?

Detmar: In all of life, information has a natural flow, and it flows to the dictum of cooperative relevancy. That is, information is directed by the consciousness to the appropriate area within a life embodied organization where the information has pertinence. In the case of an animal's body the cell retains that information and knowledge that it needs to function and adhere to its purpose. Any information extraneous to its singular purposes is passed on to appropriate places outside of it. If it is information that is vital or consequential to the rest of the body, it will be passed to the areas affected or ultimately to the brain when further or general considerations are needed.

Haskell: What about information coming to the brain first?

Detmar: That information is considered; that is, the free will will make its equational expressions and set the results against its priorities in order to make its decisions as to how to act. Its decisions ultimately will most likely involve a physical action, and it will then pass on the final information to the appropriate parts of the body that will act on the consummation of its decisional directives. All life that requires cooperation will structure a system of informational cooperative relevancy.

Haskell: This concept is not clear to me.

Detmar: If a life entity needs to cooperate with another life entity, then there will necessarily be a resultant informational exchange within the cooperative associates (organs, tissues), as an animal body is a group of associative cells, as is also a human body.

Haskell: Or to add other examples, I suppose we could consider a corporate entity such as a company that produces something for consumption, or a unit family, a government, or a club of some sort.

Detmar: Yes. Any of life's entities could be an example. When in need of cooperation with other entities, we can define some sort of cooperative body where the cohesive factor is the common information that is exchanged within the members for the purpose of promoting the groups and ultimately the individual life entity's survival. As the communicative exchange of information is necessary to enable groups to cooperate, the society forming a life group will need to be able to appropriately direct the information as efficiently as possible.

Haskell: Yes, it would.

D: Consequently, life's group entities have constructed information systems that distribute information according to this principle of cooperative relevancy. The information is distributed to the appropriate place in the group where it will be used to the greatest and most efficient advantage.

Haskell: I think I understand this principle, but perhaps an example or two would be good.

Detmar: Just as the body has a system set up within it to disseminate knowledge according to the cooperative need of the social entity, other cooperative bodies set up systems to endeavor to do the same - to pass on information according to the principle of cooperative relevancy, that is, life passes information on to the relevant areas where further cooperation will promote its survival.

Haskell: OK.

Detmar: When the individual cell amidst the life body has information introduced to it, such as, the intrusion of an inimical foreign body to its environment, its internal workings will deal with it the best way possible trying to cure the situation. If the situation is critical and the inimical influence of the foreign body or an incidence, such as, an injury or a cut is greater than the healing capabilities of the individual cell, then information is passed on, either passively or actively, to other surrounding cells which may help or to the nerve cells which will send the information to the central processor for further consideration and possible help. A system is in place that facilitates the inclusion of the other capabilities or of the rest of the association to act cohesively in order to defeat the problem, but information must be passed cooperatively throughout the system to those areas where the information is relevant to accomplish the goal. This informational dissemination system must be present in any corporate situation whether it is a single biological being or a societal confluence of many entities gathering together to attain a purpose that will promote its survival and take it up, away from misery.

Haskell: Yes, I agree.

Detmar: In a business situation where people band together to produce goods or services that will be consumed by life entities, the corporation will put together a system of information transfer and those companies that do it well will be those that prosper, given that the information is adhered to.

Haskell: Yes. I can see that this is true. When people gather together for a purpose, whether in business or pleasure, they will attempt to communicate that which is according to their purpose, and as the group becomes larger; it naturally attempts to set up lines of efficient communication the purpose of which is to pass along their information to whom it is appropriate in order to further cooperation in producing goods or services on the business level or for their societal pleasure on the social level.

Detmar: Correct.

Haskell: And where does this lead us in answering how this principle of information moving according to cooperative relevance demonstrates that the public corporation cannot do as well as the private corporation in the world's market places?

Detmar: The governmentally owned corporation unfortunately cannot set up efficient information flows according to cooperative relevance.

Haskell: How is this different from the private corporation? The political members that oversee the corporation essentially would be the board of directors and voting constituents of the republic would be its stockholders analogous to the situation of the private corporation.

Detmar: Yes, the situations are commensurate but the public company does not operate efficiently because the information is interrupted by politicos. Their purposes may be wide and varied as dictated by their various constituents, but the purpose of the private corporation is singular: it is economic; it is to make a profit resultant of producing its goods or services and to reward the stockholders for their sacrifice in their investment in the company. Unfortunately, the stockholders of the public (governmental) corporation, the constituents of the republic in which the company exists, do not, or perhaps I should say, cannot expect a dividend check at the end of each quarter albeit that they should.

Haskell: Yes. I follow this. It can be readily seen that a nationally owned corporation can be readily saddled with purposes that are politically expedient and outside the purpose of the private economic corporation.

Detmar: Consequently, the proprietary information of the company would not flow according to our dictum, generally, from its work groups upward toward management and then back down in an informational symbiosis. The public corporation would have additional directives coming from non-self promoting corporate issues coming from the agendas of the politicians overriding and interdicting that which evolves naturally within the economic animal. They would have dual interests: as a member of the board of directors on the public corporation, they would have not only the interests of the company, but also as a member of the government and a representative of their constituents, they would have their political interests in mind. This can present at times a conflict.

Chapter 6 - The Inherent Right To Property

Haskell: Detmar, you have answered all my interrogatories, but yet, I am not able to assimilate it entirely. In fact, there are even some areas of our discussion that still leave me bewildered. Although I listened and comprehended, I have not yet assimilated enough of your explanations to be able to repeat them. Further, I have no understanding of how to integrate all these explanations together.

Detmar: I see.

Haskell: For example, I am at a loss as to the significance of the issue of how the unequal and variable in society can bring forth good. I am wondering if we could go back over what we have discussed, collect the subject matter, and develop an integrated narrative of decision making in economic theory.

Detmar: Surely.

Haskell: Thank you. This will enable me to understand what has transpired today.

Detmar: Alright. We can do that.

Haskell: In fact, I hesitate to even suggest a point where this summary could commence because I feel, as Socrates espoused, that I know that I know nothing, or at least, not much.

Detmar: To start, let's go to the concept of the equation and what it represents.

Haskell: Fine.

Detmar: The equation describes life's situation: that everything we do is a sacrifice to obtain a reward. The left side of the equation is the sacrifice and the right side is the reward, that the sacrifice equals the reward even though sometimes we feel it does not, and that the sacrifice was more than the reward.

Haskell: I understand the presence of risk and the priorities on both sides which dictate that it always cannot be so.

Detmar: And the free will sets up the calculative proportions of the equation as free will is our reasoning faculties plus the life's energy itself.

Haskell: OK.

Detmar: Our equational expression represents the calculative nature of our decision making process. On the first level, we make mental decisions, and as the results of the decisions accumulate, we put the good ones into memory as priorities to be used later when making further decisions.

Haskell: Yes. These priorities are our accumulated experiences which help us make good decisions in life. It is obvious that a person with experience (and therefore knowledge) in a certain field will be more able to guide himself, others, or a company in making good decisions relevant to the accumulated experience. This is apparent in commerce and in the professional field as companies choose executives that have plenty of experience in their field, and we will always choose the experienced, knowledgeable professional when in need of advise.

Detmar: And the construction of these calculative events is done so with our survival in mind. To wit, we find ourselves existing not by our choice but with the desire to perpetuate our existence and further to do it in a way that will take us away from misery. This is our situation.

Haskell: I agree, and again, I understand that sometimes chance appears in some individuals' predicament creating a situation where there may develop an exception to the above rule. I agree it can be said that life wants to perpetuate its own existence. It seems to like to exist especially when it can eliminate misery that may be attendant to it.

Detmar: The point where we should begin is at the production of these equations and the decisions that they represent because in order to participate in life, decisions must be made and every one is performed with the relevant point of reference being the individual originating the decisional calculations.

Haskell: This sounds like it is a world of selfishness. I would like to think there is room for altruism and a little bit of thinking of the other person. I would like to believe there are a couple of nice guys around.

Detmar: The equation governs every single decision that we make; but that does not mean that we cannot be altruistic. We can act for another because of a previously established priority as dictated by the results of an equational calculation that we store in memory for later reference. This priority was calculated with internal originating experiential components including the need for cooperation weighing the equation heavily to the extent that it becomes a serious priority.

Haskell: So, as I understand it, because of this powerful feeling of cooperation, we are actually compelled by its high priority status to be altruistic or friendly or cooperative.

Detmar: Yes.

Haskell: But this picture still is not complete. Something still seems missing in order to understand this concept.

Detmar: We have cooperative priorities because of the greater priority (already established) of our will to produce cooperatively to take us away from misery. There are basic overriding priorities such as to survive and get far away from misery and to be survived by our offspring. We have internal originating experiences that the free will places into the equation and because the informative stimuli are so powerful, the calculations are easy and become high priorities for us.

Haskell: So, I agree that we want to execute these

enumerated priorities and perhaps others as well. But so what? It still does not clarify my problem of understanding the existence of altruism or easier yet, just being friendly. Is it just because we want to produce, and so, we are cooperative? What about Sidney Carton?

Detmar: There are two types of cooperative behavior - social and economic. Economic cooperation indicates that we want to cooperate for the purpose of exchanging one thing for another. When we socialize with a friend, we cooperate but without a view to obtain an economic return on our cooperation. The social return we seek is to be able to enjoy the companionship of another.

Haskell: And altruism?

Detmar: Altruism is the sacrifice we make for an internally originating return only. We do not expect a return from outside of ourselves or from any other person. We do it only for our own internal gratification whatever it may be. We may make a sacrifice for our offspring that may promote their survival.

Haskell: And the altruism of Sydney Carton?

Detmar: "It is a far, far better thing that I do, than

I have ever done..." He uses the word "better". In Carton's view he is sacrificing himself at the hands of his executioner to promote somebody else's survival. He does it because he knows that the other person will do good in this world, and he knows that he, himself, has not been productive and is dissatisfied with what he has done, or not done, and naturally, as he put it, "it is a far, far better thing that I do..." He performed the sacrifice of laying down his life - the ultimate altruistic behavior - because he felt productive this way and it gave him self-gratification. All our actions of sacrifice have an objective of some sort of return. If there is no return, the behavioral action is an aberration. Even Jesus, as altruistic as any man in history, had an objective.

Haskell: What about just going out onto one's porch on a pleasant Sunday afternoon and just basking on a lawn chair in the sun in total relaxation.

Detmar: In order to be able to arrange the opportunity to put one's self in that situation we had to do many actions or toils to prepare ourselves for the event of going out onto the porch. We had to work to save the money to buy the house and the lawn chair and to set aside the short period of time when we take a break from working to go out onto the porch and just relax and enjoy the day. We sacrificed ourselves in working hard at our jobs to obtain the return of the enjoyment of our deck on the house.

Haskell: I see. So all our behavior is sacrificial to obtain a return and our basic equational expression covers this situation.

Detmar: Yes.

Haskell: And even the behavior of a nice guy is sacrificial in nature. The nice guy is nice because, first, he enjoys being cooperative on the economic and social level, and secondly, he has established a priority that he enjoys seeing others do well. It is because of an internally originating experience which he has calculated, prioritized, and incorporated into his life style.

Detmar: Correct.

Haskell: And where do we go from here in our summary? I have retained and comprehended some of today's interview, and I would think that perhaps we should go to the next level of the sacrificial decision by adding in physical effort to the equational expression.

Detmar: Yes, but previous to that we need to

continue a bit our inquiry into the primary expression and its implications.

Haskell: Surely.

Detmar: We noted that the life entity has no choice in its suddenly finding itself living, existing; and it quickly establishes the first priority for itself that it would like to continue to live, avoid misery, and prosper.

Haskell: Even a simple life form wants to continue living and do what it does.

Detmar: Yes. As this situation was given to the entity, that is, life did not construct this situation for itself, we awoke to find ourselves existing one day. Somehow the situation for life developed in order to support the existence of a sentience.

Haskell: And I remember in our third disquisition on truth, decisions, and free will, the notes of which I published, that we established that in order for this situation to arise knowledge was needed to enable the molecules to reorder themselves and begin to produce life generating actions. Because of the second law of thermodynamics that the universe tends toward entropy, in order to reverse this situation (which life does) knowledge is required by molecules in order to make a decision. A decision is impossible without knowledge, and hence, it appears in our equational expression.

Detmar: Correct. And hence, because of the pre-existence of knowledge, we owe our existence not to ourselves, but to something before us that provided the anti-entropic knowledge.

Haskell: Yes, I agree.

Detmar: Thus, the components to our equational description of decision making are owed to a creator previous to our existence and then, secondly, to ourselves.

Haskell: I see where you are going: you are concluding that we own our effort, time, and information or that it belongs to our creator.

Detmar: That is right. It was bequeathed to us by virtue of the birth of our consciousness, and then, we are given the overwhelming interior originating experience of the desire to continue to live which we prioritize highly. Of course, due to the existence of risk there occasionally appears an exception later on in an entity's life compelling it to suicide. But this is the exception due to the existential nature of the risk of living in this world.

Haskell: Agreed. What has been done here is the establishment of the inherent right to property: the primary rights exist with our creator and secondarily with ourselves. We have been given existence and a supply of interior originating experiences that inform us, or should I say, compel us to prioritize our life to strive to continue to live; and in order to carry out this situation we need to allow our free will to apply effort to effect our sacrifices that we need to make in order to accomplish this directive.

Detmar: Yes, and wholesale summary interference in this process is unnatural and wrong.

Haskell: The obvious conclusion of this is that collectivization and the negation of property rights is immoral.

Detmar: Correct. It cannot be usurped by the society in which the entity lives without first the acquiescence of the individual contractually conveying its own right to its effort to the group's ownership.

Haskell: And of course, we have already established that the extrapolation of effort is to property and material capital goods. Property such as land, capital goods, and consumer goods are an extension of effort.

Detmar: Right.

Haskell: To sum up what we have so far is that we find ourselves existing, and we need to deal with it by making decisions in order to effectuate our survival. The means to perform this task pre-exist us, and hence, devolve to us for our own use.

Detmar: Good.

Chapter 7 - The Law Of Differentiation

Haskell: And when we make a mental decision to do something, our free will uses time, information previously established knowledge, and mental effort amidst an environment of risk to make the decision. When that mental decision becomes manifested in a physical action to obtain a return, we include the component of physical action to both sides of the equations. We add it to the left side to denote the physical decision to do something, and we add this component to the right side to denote the physical nature of the good or service of that which we are working to obtain which will promote our survival.

Detmar: Good.

Haskell: Further, when we add in the cooperative nature of societal man seeking to exchange what we can do for each other in terms of goods and services (which are essentially the same thing), we get an exchange between participants, and this exchange is perceived to be to the betterment of each participant.

Haskell: And we express this exchange by equating the sacrifice of one to the other.

Detmar: The reason why the exchange comes to be is that it is more efficient than if the participants were to attempt to obtain the returns of their sacrifices by themselves individually. The nature of all product and service efficiency is through the enhancement of one of the ingredients to our equational expression, id est, time, risk, effort or particularly the accumulation of knowledge. When one person acquires more knowledge than another in the area of the production of something, he can become more efficient when we effect the effort to make the sacrifice and consummate the production of something. Naturally, as people acquire more knowledge in certain areas than others, they become better at what they do, and this accumulation of knowledge leads to specializing in producing those things of which they hold this knowledge.

Haskell: But the environment is part of our ability to produce things, especially for a farmer producing his crops and livestock. A farmer in a conducive environment will be better able to grow certain crops in one area as opposed to another. Is this in our equation?

Detmar: The environment is the spatial reference through which passes the influences of the components of our equational expression. In a certain relevant area over time and at a certain probability (or risk factor), effort and knowledge in the consciousness are combined by the free will to apply energy in a certain way to produce a reward for us that will help the sentient being survive. It does not matter that the effort and knowledge work on something that is material (a product) or energetic (a service) because the purpose of both are the same - to help improve our condition. Just as in physics which ultimately instructs us that matter and energy are the same (interchangeable), in economics the nature of the product and service are ultimately the same. It does not matter whether we decide to produce a fan to make us cool on a hot day or we hire a person to fan us, the purpose was to get air to pass over us to make us comfortable.

Haskell: You spoke just a bit ago about the natural variation in the manufacturing and accumulation of knowledge. Let's go over the nature of variation and its goodness again.

Detmar: Science knows that variation is produced by risk and the environment's influence on us, and in reproductive matters variation is produced by recombination of genetic material and by the risk of the actions involved in the recombination.

Haskell: Yes.

Detmar: This diversity is needed because uniformity is a disaster and inefficient by itself. If we were to be all the same, then we would be equal in every pursuit, and it would be difficult for society to differentiate, and hence, grow. In order for society to become more efficient in production, accumulation of knowledge is needed. The division of labor is nothing else but a concentration and accumulation of knowledge more than others in a singular area. Physical effort and time are the same, and risk decreases because of the further application of the new knowledge.

Haskell: Yes. I know that biological anthropologists proselytize about the value of variation in evolution. It seems obvious to me that if everyone were a mathematician or an English professor or a sportsman or a tradesman or whatever, there would be a deficiency in other areas to keep society operating at its current level of productivity. We need a variation of skills and proclivities to fill the sundry needs of society and certainly to fill the requirements presented by the division of labor. I think it is pretty clear that variation is good.

Detmar: Yes.

Haskell: You just mentioned that the origin of efficiency and the division of labor is primarily in the accumulation of knowledge. Let's talk about this a little more.

Detmar: To give an example, looking back to our situation with the farmer considering the inclusion of the potato farmer from across the river, we should note that in order for the farmer to start his production of legumes, he needs the implementation of potato horticultural knowledge into the equational expression providing an answer that prompts our farmer to plant. It is knowledge that he can grow them and that they are beneficial to him and others in nutritional value.

Haskell: OK.

Detmar: And because of his conclusion that it is worth it for him to produce potatoes, he will inductively reason that it will have worth also to others. If he perceives that others do not have potatoes, then he knows that there should be an opportunity for a trading of production, and thus, a trading of benefits of the sacrifices.

Haskell: This is the situation where there is no competition. Hence, knowledge that you have a new product and its benefits seem obvious. But what about the case of where there are others producing the same product? Is efficiency still entirely linked to knowledge? It seems to me that we might just put more effort into it to sell our product and establish a market niche.

Detmar: More effort is not an efficiency, the definition of which should be an increase in production without a corresponding increase in effort, risk, or time.

Haskell: Hence, according to our equational expression only an increase in information/knowledge or a decrease in risk or time would fit this definition, and probably, most of the reductions in risk would still be the result of an involvement of knowledge about risk.

Detmar: Yes, when there are others producing the same product, the same principles apply: a greater accumulation of knowledge and a decrease in risk will serve as the determining factors in whose products will become prominent in the marketplace and which companies will survive and prosper.

Haskell: How?

Detmar: All efficiency is producing more with the same or less, assuming risk is the same over time (exempli gratia, force majeure) and all other risk is technologically controllable. Hence, efficiency is a sub-category of growth, and growth we know to be any increase in production by any cause, and efficiency being improvement in the equational factors. By the free will, which is our will (life's energy) plus the reasoning faculties, we look to improve our knowledge. We apply this improved knowledge to our effort. Capital is an outgrowth of effort, and knowledge, therefore, can be said to be the progenitor of capital improvement, and thus, every efficiency we undergo.

Haskell: I see, and it applies whether an inventor is bringing out a new product that will improve our lives or a company improves upon a product to make it better than its competitor's; in each case the improvement is generated from knowledge.

Detmar: Yes. The creativity of the free will enables us to increase our knowledge, and when this knowledge is employed to decrease either the risk, time, or effort factors and transfer any of this decreased increment to the capital factor, an efficiency occurs.

Haskell: Interesting. So, the essence of efficiency is the transference of any quantity of the equational factors to the capital coefficient which emanates from effort, and this transference is accomplished by the free will being applied to the available information and knowledge.

Detmar: To further the summary, the components of growth are efficiency plus differentiation.

Haskell: I do not understand.

Detmar: Efficiency is any improvement in the equational components; and so, more can be produced with fewer encumbrances; this allows the individual or group to use the new found resources (for example, more available effort and time, with less risk) to differentiate into other occupations.

Haskell: And a natural objective would be to pursue an increase of knowledge to understand what vocation to which to go or in what area one needs to place his personal assets.

Detmar: Correct. And the increase of knowledge is improved through a variation which directs our interests throughout the realm. As diversification develops, a preponderancy of knowledge is developed since each interest pursues knowledge further in that area.

Haskell: I understand.

Detmar: And just as the variation and diversity in knowledge improve the growth and efficiency of productive society, inequality within the abilities of man improves our standard of living.

Haskell: When you speak of inequality, you are referring to actually just variation and diversity.

Detmar: It is the same. One is unequal due to the combination of risk (the environment) with the variation or diversity within the life entity's categorical group (to wit, the species).

Haskell: And thusly, even though there are those within a categorical group that are not equal in one way or another, this diversity is ultimately good because although not everyone is a mathematical or physics genius - I certainly am not - almost everyone does have a proclivity or talent that will lend itself well to help in the production of something in one way or another. Because we have diversity, we have the various proclivities and capacities that allow for a society to generate the various products that it needs to survive and particularly to take it away from misery in as diverse a fashion as possible.

Detmar: That's right.

Haskell: And let's review the argument against mercantilism.

Detmar: When a country does not allow certain imports for protectionist purposes, it is basically not allowing an efficiency from without to enter. And if it does not allow a good (or service) such as a medicine or a high capacity machine to enter, it does not allow its economy to be as totally efficient as it could be.

Haskell: Sure. The machine would allow the society to make more of something with less effort. The medicine would allow the people of the society to enjoy greater health allowing it less down time from sickness and obviously promoting survival.

Detmar: Yes.

Haskell: However, is it always an "efficiency"? I can understand the use of the word "efficiency" to denote the situation where another or outside area or entity produces a better medicine or machine that performs in a better capacity, but what about an example of a more mundane good such as designer clothes or just blue jeans?

Detmar: If the potential importing country, that does not have the designer clothes or the "hip" blue jeans, allows not the importation of these type of items, it is because it does not have the capacity to produce these types of trend setting, fashionable products that some people would demand and that another country is more efficient at producing; but mercantilistic policy tries to negate this demand and supplant it with a supply that is inferior.

Haskell: But does it matter to the economic society if it does not allow such items that seemingly are not as important as other products in other market sectors such as health, bio-technology, construction et al?

Detmar: Although excluding vainglorious products from a society for reasons of mercantilism does not harm the physical health of a society, it still has an impact. If the society's consumers would prefer one line of products to another, then to a certain degree their happiness is impinged somewhat by the mercantilistic rules. And hence, the efficiency to producing happiness and taking us away from misery is lessened.

Haskell: But what if this vaingloriousness is no good for a society; perhaps, it is best not to be allowed into a society.

Detmar: If you are referring to an electorate democratically deciding against products, such as drugs that are prone to usage abuse, then it is the will of the people with all their collective free will being applied to the problem. If you are speaking of some governmental edict or rules generated by an elitist bureaucrat or politician, that has decided because he is or they are know-it-alls and that they have decided what is best for all people, then we need to review why such elitist behavior does not work.

Haskell: I recall earlier in this conversation that we showed when decisions are made and planned centrally, the amount of free will available to decisional equations is less, and hence, overall the quality of production and life will fall.

Detmar: That is it, exactly.

Haskell: Let us bring up another question now that I am thinking about it. We seem to be implying that the only thing important in society is production, that producing goods and services are the only things that matter in society. Surely, there are other concerns that are important to us, especially in the area of cerebral and aesthetic matters.

Detmar: All decisions result in a sacrifice for a purpose. When we decide to do something we make a sacrifice in order to obtain a result. Our sacrifice can be to obtain a material thing that will make our life less miserable and further us toward happiness, such as a car, a television, a house, or medicine. It, of course, can be anything that we would wish and strive for. But the sacrifice may also be non-material for our cerebral pleasure exclusively.

Haskell: Yes, for example we sacrifice our time in order to read a book for cerebral pleasure. Or the ascetic monk makes a sacrifice by the banishment of all material things from his life in order that he might reach a stage of enlightenment.

Detmar: And this sacrificing of time and effort for the satisfying result of the aesthetic or cerebral pleasure that is derived from the book or other is equivalent to the production of a good in order to enjoy its use.

Haskell: I see. The overall equation is the Sacrifice

which hopefully equals the result, and this decisional situation can be narrowed to the production of a specific objective.

Detmar: Correct.

Haskell: Let's get back to our subject of mercantilism and how it is not an efficient strategy.

Detmar: It is because if the markets are denied goods that would otherwise be present, then the market economy is not as efficient as it could be in taking us away from misery and delivering us the best opportunity for the highest standard of living. A common governmental and regulatory worry is that if there is a free flow of goods across borders, jobs will be displaced.

Haskell: Yes, although they will be displaced, will it overall be good for society, for I know that in one sense there is an overall improvement in efficiency, but I am not convinced that means an absolute overall good and improvement will requisitely follow?

Detmar: It follows because there is an insistent generation of sacrifices to promote goodness.

Haskell: I do not follow you at all.

Detmar: Let us go back to our second dialogue on ethics where we realized that the good is that which promotes survival and takes us away from misery. To this we note that we have coming to our consciousness an interior originating experience that informs us of a desire to make these sacrifices to produce good, and our free will loads this experience into the equation, and we calculate. As it happens to be a strong and constant proclivity for us, we place it high on our priority list.

Haskell: In other words we have the constant desire to produce and make sacrifices to produce goods and services in order to live and better ourselves. But what does this have to do with mercantilism?

Detmar: The problem we are seeking to understand is whether a governmental or regulatory edict banning the importation of anything and promoting indigenous manufacture and exportation has any advantage over free trade.

Haskell: Yes. It is as if I am asking which is better for the overall societal good: free trade, or partial or selective trade.

Detmar: Leaving aside the issue of a society sometimes eliminating certain goods that it deems harmful such as opium, we propound that free trade is a more efficient vehicle to promote the general societal weal because of its overall efficiency. However, when an efficiency is introduced from abroad and incorporated into society, sometimes the new capital good or service will displace the labor organization of a society in essence putting somebody out of their job.

Haskell: Yes. This is the crux.

Detmar: It should be seen that it is no different from the same problem within a corporate society: that is, if an invention such as a large commercial oven makes the manufacture of bread easier and it allows the baker to not use so many helpers in his baking of the loaves everyday for shipment to the stores, it is analogous to the question of whether the corporation should install the new technological devise and have no need for the superfluous employees. Or let us say that a machine comes onto the market that makes bread production very easy and cheap. We see people go to the store to invest in one of these machines in order to self-manufacture the bread making the need for some bakers and baker helpers less pressing. Suddenly, some bakers and their helpers will not be needed by society as much as before. Of course, we have seen that a company that is investing in new equipment often is expanding and able to transfer the employees to openings in other corporate operations.

Haskell: Yes, this is an actual circumstance, and we can visualize the situation of the capital good being invented and produced either abroad or here. The result is the same: there is some displacement of labor. For my part, I see that the trend of the free introduction of these capital devices is good because it allows for greater efficiency in the production of bread and permits people to pursue the obtainment and enjoyment of bread more easily and more efficiently. It lowers the cost of the bread making it more obtainable to more people. I see clearly that the introduction of the capital good which is nothing else but an efficiency is a betterment and a boon for society. And, I see that history shows us that we have advanced and have a society that makes it easier for us to survive and prosper than before. Clearly, this century has produced marvelous advances over last century.

Detmar: The introduction of efficiency takes precedence over displacement of labor. The originator of the equations is the free will, holder of our creativity, and there is a constant impetus of the free will to promote the production of these equations and this is eminently seen, prima facie, by the advancement of mankind over its history.

Haskell: OK.

Detmar: The effectuation of the mental equations is decisions many of which come to be priorities which are a type of knowledge. When we add physical effort to the equations, they result in the physical production of goods and services (which we have noted are the same thing).

Haskell: Yes. These equations are the representations of our decisional behavior.

Detmar: And the capital efficiencies are in competition with labor within these decisional equations.

Haskell: How's that?

Detmar: When the free will introduces an efficiency, which we will call a capital efficiency, into the equation, it harbors less effort or time needed to make the sacrifice in producing something. (Remember, an efficiency is the transference of any quantity of the equational factors to the capital factor.) Thus, an available quantity of effort or time can be allotted elsewhere in the economy of the individual being a single equation; or if a society, it would be an agglomeration of equations which could be summarized by adding up the several to one all inclusive equation.

Haskell: I think I see.

Detmar: This available effort or time is an additional resource which can be placed elsewhere for production purposes further elevating us away from misery.

Haskell: This actually means that when an efficiency is introduced to society and utilized by a corporate manufacturer that, if there is a displacement of labor, this is actually beneficial to the company and society in general. Displacement of labor through the introduction of a capital efficiency from wherever is actually a good thing! We should look to the opportunity to generate any extra, superfluous labor time.

Detmar: Further, our decisions are governed by the equational expressions, and we have established that all capital is established from free will operating on the components, id est, risk, time, effort, and information. When it comes to capital creation, as risk over time is for all practical purposes a constant, only information and effort vary widely for the situation of capital creation. The purpose of capital and effort is to produce more; hence, we attach the appearance of capital to effort as a coefficient, all capital being an efficiency. These goods and services are all meant to help us survive and take us away from misery.

Haskell: Interesting. All capital is created by this free will acting upon knowledge and effort.

Detmar: And wealth is measured by the possessions, or the potential to possess things, to wit, goods and services, or something else, such as knowledge itself. So, we may conclude that the origin of all wealth over time is through previous or current knowledge, opportunity (risk), and effort.

Haskell: Really?

Detmar: If society witnesses the payment of a high salary to a company executive and a very low wage to a clerk, it is because the executive has amassed considerable knowledge along with the will to effectuate it through effort and the opportunity to be present.

Haskell: So all wealth is backed by risk, knowledge, and effort?

Detmar: Since capital is a coefficient or extension of effort, we may say that all wealth is backed by risk (the opportunity to take advantage of the situation), knowledge, effort-capital, and time.

Haskell: OK.

Detmar: We also know that an efficiency is originated by the free will creating knowledge enabling the transference of quantities from risk, effort, time to capital goods and services; capital, that is not yet converted to goods and services, is money - money being promissory notes indicating the right to present or future production.

Haskell: Hence, we may conclude that when an efficiency is excluded from society's potential, wealth is excluded and its reservoir of knowledge and differentiation is less than it otherwise could be, and thus, a mercantilistic society will be lacking in knowledge and in displaced and differentiating effort, assuming the risk and time are consistent.

Haskell: Wait. Does the importation of the good or service equate itself to knowledge? If a country does not allow a pair of blue jeans to pass its borders, then surely we cannot say that the country lacks in knowledge.

Detmar: We can because that blue jean has something of it that appeals to consumers; and knowledge and effort were the original instruments that created the blue jean. It could be the style of the blue jean, it could be the material makeup; or it could be the name value or possibly something else. Even name value comes from the experience of the manufacturer developing and marketing its product over time, and this knowledge self-develops a name by which its constituents could recognize and appreciate for whatever reason.

Haskell: Thus, we should conclude that mercantilism will always fail ultimately when in direct comparison to the open free trade society, unless, of course, it is blessed with a huge quantity of natural resources or some other off-setting circumstance provided by opportunity which we understand to be of the risk component.

Detmar: It will not be as efficient as an open trade society. The same principle applies with local trade or at the international trade level; it is not as efficient as free trade quantitatively, and hence, over time the efficiencies of the free market will always overtake the economic mercantilistic society.

Haskell: Let's go further along in our summary. The economic transaction is when the supply side priority is lowered to meet the demand side priority and is described by R X T X E X I/K = The Sacrifice of the seller which equals the R X T X E X I/K of the buyer.

Detmar: Correct.

Haskell: And how would we describe competition?

Detmar: Competition is the relationship of the supply side of the equational expression with the other substitutive demand side equations' portions. As we just mentioned, the priority of the supply side comes down searching for the beginning of the demand side of the equation. Once these priorities meet, initiation of the transactions begins. If the demand side is more plentiful, there will be at the bottom of the priority scale a dearth of product as the production quantities were exhausted earlier on with those transactions of the demand side that had the highest priority. Should this happen, the prices will rise as an aggregate because the equations with the lower priorities will have to increase the priority level in order to reach for product now allowed by the new higher paying level permitted by their new higher priority,

Haskell: I see. And the opposite would be true if the supply side has greater production than the demand side requires: all the priorities would be covered and this information would come to the higher prioritized equations, and they would adjust by downgrading their established priorities toward the lower end until the extra production meets the priorities of the demand side. And as the supply side priorities pull new demand side priorities up which did not allow the individual buyer previously to come to the market, these new consumers will now be allowed to enter and acquire some supply.

Detmar: Yes.

Haskell: But you mentioned that the law of supply and demand is not a law but a general indicative rule at best because price does not always perfectly correlate in the classical sense. One of the possible explanations is known as the elasticity of demand.

Detmar: It does not follow perfectly because the law does not allow for the several variables of the equational expression particularly the priority within the component of knowledge. There is time, risk, effort and knowledge; albeit, the time and risk factors do not change much over the long run, but they can influence the short run severely.

Haskell: OK. But we still have not gotten to the explanation of how competition works.

Detmar: It is the relationship of the available and relevant equations on the supply side to the available and relevant equations on the demand side en masse.

Haskell: Elaborate, please.

Detmar: First, I say "relevant" because competition means or indicates a conflict of interest. In the business sense it is the conflict of selling the same capital product (which is, as we have noted, a good or a service) to the same demand entity.

Haskell: And this will lower prices, or I should say, usually will lower the price.

Detmar: The price lowers because of our law of differentiation.

Haskell: What is that? You have mentioned that we can differentiate out of the original components of the equation other factors and coefficients from the information/knowledge factor, and I believe the sense of use is similar to the way the mathematician might use the word in referring to the calculative methods in calculus.

Detmar: The law of differentiation asseverates that life strives to lessen conflicts and eliminate its struggles, and this carries into the sphere of economics. It does this by differentiating, that is, it seeks to make itself different from others by attempting to make its products somehow unique having its own niche in the marketplace. Companies, even though they may be in the same general business, seek a singular place in the market where they alone rest.

Haskell: I have a couple of doubts about this. First is that life does not necessarily seek to dissolve its conflicts. What about war? History is full of it. These wars come from somewhere. First, there is peace, and then, there is war. Secondly, economically speaking, companies are constantly invading the economic niches of others causing direct conflict.

Detmar: War is born of politics. In every case there exists an ideological conflict within the mind of the political establishment that it believes is compelling enough to create physical strife. And since political leaders are individuals, the physical strife is born of conflicts generated by the problems within the minds of a few. Often in history we have seen the political mind corrupt itself and degenerate into extreme selfishness producing an evil agenda which cascades into the wholesale generation of misery. As the very origin of the misery lies in a conflict of a selfish mind, its concept of that which is good becomes distorted, and hence, so does the perception of its objectives and the conflicts or problems which it must solve.

Haskell: It would be interesting indeed if tomes were to be written exploring this in historical terms, but go ahead and elaborate a bit how this theory of the separation of conflicts exists in the economic arena.

Detmar: It exists in economics because it exists in the life entity. That which lives wants to better itself and the lives of those who will survive it, and it does so by cooperating with those around it for the purposes of executing the completion of its sacrifices that are its objectives in surviving and avoiding misery and promoting happiness.

Haskell: Wait. There are a few objections to the life entity's desideratum to avoid conflicts. First would be the example of sports where athletes purposefully engage in direct conflict with each other; and secondly, I have seen people, particularly young boys, directly place themselves in conflict and even instigate a confrontation looking for trouble. Thus, although I see that maybe, generally, life entities try to avoid conflict, it does not seem a universal truism.

Detmar: As for the young tough, he puts himself in harm's way for the pure enjoyment of it, and the consequences of such behavior often become irrelevant, or at least subordinated, to the pleasure of the excitement it affords.

Haskell: So?

Detmar: Our statement of differentiation refers to a decision to reach a specific sacrifice that has the objective of generating production for the purpose of survival.

Haskell: But the young tough sacrifices the consequences of his behavior to realize the thrill of the action of the conflict. It is the sacrificial result of a decision and its production is pleasure.

Detmar: Yes, it is, but the means to the end here are the same. The confrontation is part of the objective here and the laws of differentiation and conflict avoidance is preserved because the combatant, whether it is the tough or the athlete, looks to avoid conflict that will have the potential to interrupt his confrontation or inhibit playing in his game.

Haskell: You are right. The athlete will definitely look to avoid conflict on his way to the competition and the perpetrator will tend to avoid the police before, during, and after the confrontation, illicit or not.

Detmar: The same stands true for the economic situation. Any entity that looks to produce a capital good (this, of course, includes a service) will always look to differentiate.

Haskell: It still seems that I do not yet understand this differentiation law yet. I recognize that probably companies want to avoid direct competition, but I know also that sometimes companies move out of their product lines and expand into others, and consequently, come into direct contact with another company and its product line. As a matter of fact, I have had the experience of attending and walking a trade show where there were, literally, thousands of vendors displaying their wares to potential professional buyers in the retail industry, and I can assuredly say that there was significant duplication of product. How can this be consistent with your hypothesis that life entities, and particularly companies, look to avoid conflict and confrontation?

Detmar: Although there is duplication of product and at your trade show there were many vendors that seemingly were in direct competition with each other, it still does not impinge on the integrity of the statement because the law states that they tend toward singularity of the economic niche. That is, they constantly search for ways to make themselves different which in their parlance they would describe their situation as becoming "more competitive."

Haskell: The term "more competitive" means the same thing as "differentiation"?

Detmar: One form of differentiation is the process of becoming more competitive. Just as species of flora or fauna settle into ecological niches, companies will differentiate in many ways to make themselves singular in the marketplace carving themselves an economic niche, if you will, constructing brand names, using research to develop new products that will give themselves a new place or give them a lead in the market.

Haskell: I see. Marketing, research, sales, and quality are all examples of differentiation.

Detmar: And efficiency which reduces costs making a capital product less expensive is a big differentiation that is the focal point of a good company. When a company comes into a niche for the first time with existing product already there, it is because the managers of the corporation have decided that, although their products are similar, they will be able to produce it at less cost, or with better quality, or the niche is not full yet and the existing companies, there, have not adequately marketed their products to the fullest extent possible within that niche. The company believes that they have already differentiated because they perceive that their costs are lower, that they have a competitive advantage, that they are in a different and better situation to bring their products to the marketplace.

Haskell: But sometimes, don't some companies go ahead into direct competition anyway?

Detmar: If they do, they would do so due to the element of risk in that people make mistakes all the time, and we note this with the inclusion of the component of risk. But the more developed life entities are, the more cognizant they are of their situation, and the more they will understand their need to differentiate into a niche whether it be a geographical or economic niche.

Haskell: Why though? Why is it necessary for the life entity to follow such a course?

Detmar: To decrease risk. The more the life entity comes up against direct competitive situations and involves itself in the problems of conflict of interests, the more risk is amplified in his life increasing the possibility of loss or failure. There is no escaping the reality of risk: if it accumulates in an entity's life, it increases the chance of failure. Life understands this and naturally will want to avoid the possibility of failure.

Haskell: Interesting, and a remarkable conclusion: the existence of risk dictates the law of life's will to differentiate.

Detmar: Indubitably.

Haskell: Well, how do we express symbolically in an equational expression the nature of competition or the free market system?

Detmar: I am glad you used the words "free market system," as "competition" should not be used because, as we have explored, the more self-cognizant a life entity is, the more its modus operandi tends to deviate from competition by searching for a niche. The species searches for its ecological niche; the individual organism searches for its geographical niche to carry on with its own life; the human individual searches for its particular job that will allow it to produce so that it can provide for himself and his family, and a group of individuals that gather together making a company produce in unison will seek its place in the market which we can say will be its market niche.

Haskell: Sometimes, a company can grow very large and dominate a marketplace, and the government will try to break it up saying that it is a monopoly. As we know here in the U.S., we have laws that try to prevent monopolistic situations from developing, and the U.S. government has an obvious policy of thwarting monopolies from occurring. Is this good and how does this policy relate to our present discussion?

Detmar: We have seen that when the company's establishes the priority of its goods, it is higher than the initial priority on the demand side. If there is a reasonable alternative for the demand side, the gap between the two priorities will be prevented from becoming too large.

Haskell: Hence, it is good to have some competition in the marketplace.

Detmar: Yes. It is good for the demand side of the equation to have alternatives, and this helps with the equalization of the priorities. It also prevents the companies from becoming stagnant in the differentiation process which generates the need to constantly pursue further efficiencies.

Haskell: Well, let me not side track you any longer regarding my inquiry into how to express this in modular terms.

Detmar: The core of the expression of the free market system is our basic modular equation that denotes the single transaction. To this we must note the process of the priorities on the supply and the demand side aligning themselves. We can express it by saying that the difference in the quantification of the Reward as measured over time on the supply side must be equal to that on the demand side. We could write this as dRwd(supply)/dt R X T X (Cy)E X I/K(priority supply side) = dRwd(demand)/dt R X T X (Cx)E X I/K(priority demand side).

Haskell: OK.

Detmar: And when considering the many equations that a market would produce, we would describe it as the difference between all the transactions over time: hence, it could be described dR(sum of transactions)/dt; and we can take the last transaction and call that the market price and the summary of the market because, after all, the latest price of the product is the summary of the product at the last moment that the market was active.

Haskell: But we used this equation already, and I was under the impression that it is not enough to describe competition, or should I say, the free market system. What about the Law of Differentiation; should it be incorporated into our modular equational expression somehow?

Detmar: You are right. This present expression describes the competitive situation where the products being chosen by the demand side are the same, and to this, we need to add the Law of Differentiation.

Haskell: As we discussed, the free market is noted as our equational expression measured over time, and its dynamics mainly rest with the priorities of the supply side narrowing the gap with those of the demand side. Naturally, the supply side of the equation starts with the higher priority making the calculation higher; and hence, the price commences greater than the demand side would like to see it. But if there is no alternative, this price may be paid by the demand side to meet its needs should the demand side priorities rise to meet it. Further, as the supply side realizes potentialities causing an increase in demand, it may lower the price to meet the priority level of a greater demand sided population which could lower its costs and raise profits. This situation is covered in economic texts.

Detmar: And you said that "the dynamics mainly rest with the priorities" because the other factors of the equation could also effect the situation.

Haskell: Yes, and I understand that the Law of Differentiation says that life entities do not like competition and that they try to avoid it.

Detmar: This law indicates that the Free Will will always endeavor to differentiate in the face of competition by willfully and purposefully using its intellectual powers to differentiate any of the components of the equation to run from the conflicts of interest that it faces. There are sundry and many consequences from the law such as changing the quality of the products or the price, the type, the variations of the products and even the invention of new products from the advent or increase of research that companies initiate in order to fulfill the law.

Haskell: Yes. The law seems responsible for all variation for which the life entity strives which hopefully produces mostly positive results, but, of course, due to the existence of risk - and I would imagine sometimes incompetence - it may not always be successful.

Detmar: But the important part is that the entity strives to the objective of positive variation that will help it survive and bring it up, away from misery.

Haskell: And can this law be incorporated into our mathematically modular equational expression?

Detmar: It is a priority: a byte of knowledge which reminds the life entity that it must avert the risk of direct conflict, and thus, a derivative of the Information-Knowledge component. As a priority, it had already been calculated by the Free Will and established as important.

Haskell: I see.

Detmar: We must add it as another component of the equation, as a derivative of the Information-Knowledge factor. It is a measure of the competence of the free will to handle the situation of the conflict of interest that presents itself to the life entity in the face of either the environment or another life entity entering its positional situation and presenting a problem to its life. The mental faculties of the entity must make a decision and it does this by calculating the Sacrifice necessary in order to resolve the matter before it. This process will result in either direct conflict and the destruction of the problem before it, or it will differentiate. The life entity will differentiate first unless that is a failure and the calculations indicate that direct conflict attendant with its risk and deleterious consequences is the only other alternative.

Haskell: I see where this has gone, but I am not yet totally convinced because I still have doubts that life entities try to differentiate first in all cases. It still seems that some of histories' great villains have gone to destruction first.

Detmar: Some have, as we talked about this in previous conversations, but it is due to the risk inherent in life. Due to the existence of risk in the universe, there are exceptions at every level even at the micro-inanimate level as demonstrated by the Heisenberg Uncertainty Principle of physics. We can extend this concept into the animate world also as it certainly exists here too. And we can conclude that due to our life relevant uncertainty principle that invokes the necessary intrusion of risk and chaos everywhere the Law of Differentiation does not always appear to be primary in life.

Haskell: Detmar, this concludes my questions, and I appreciate your help in clearing up these issues which have puzzled me. I expect I will put what I have learned today down on paper, and perhaps, it may well lend understanding to the nature of decisions and basic economic theory.

Detmar: You are welcome, and it was my pleasure to assist in this understanding.

Haskell: Thanks again, Detmar. I am sure I'll be back again to see you soon.

Detmar: Stop by anytime, Haskell. It is always a pleasure.

Haskell: Good day.